A FUTURE FOR THE PAST

A FUTURE
FOR THE PAST

MOULTRIE R. KELSALL
and
STUART HARRIS
A.R.I.B.A., A.R.I.A.S.

OLIVER AND BOYD
EDINBURGH AND LONDON
1961

OLIVER AND BOYD
Tweeddale Court
Edinburgh 1

39A Welbeck Street
London W.1

FIRST PUBLISHED 1961

PRINTED IN GREAT BRITAIN FOR OLIVER AND BOYD LTD.
BY ROBERT CUNNINGHAM AND SONS LTD., LONGBANK WORKS, ALVA

Preface

This is a book written in wrath and hope – wrath at the monumental wastage of old buildings that goes on in Scotland today: hope that it may yet be possible to stop it by marshalling the overwhelming arguments for reconstruction and showing how a satisfactory reconstruction may be achieved. To describe the wastage as monumental is no exaggeration. Its extent and rapidity, the pertinacity with which it is prosecuted, and the fact that many of the buildings destroyed are monuments to the good building tradition of an earlier Scotland, more than justify the adjective.

For anyone with a true regard for our country, travelling anywhere in it today is made tragic and infuriating by the senseless destruction evident upon all sides. You cannot go far on any road without seeing the demolition of well-built old houses in progress: if, on a journey, you happen to notice some particularly attractive stone cottage, or group of them, with neatly curtained windows and whitened door steps, you are quite likely, on passing that way a few months later, to find only an untidy heap of rubble. That is not an exaggerated statement, but one which the most casual observation will confirm. Among our humbler domestic buildings, the more comely they are, the more likely are they to be swept away. It is hard to avoid the conclusion that the very qualities which make them an ornament to the Scottish scene, and which should safeguard them, make them the special objects of attack.

The purpose of this book is to show good reason why such buildings should be saved, to show that they can be brought back into useful service to the community, and to show how this can be done. We are not primarily concerned with buildings of outstanding architectural merit or historic interest, because there is evidence of a growing public opinion opposed to their destruction, though it must still grow a great deal if that opposition is to be fully effective. Our immediate concern is for the ever-more-rapidly diminishing body of humbler and simpler buildings which, though lacking individual pretensions, are collectively a monument no less important to a once strong native building tradition which we have virtually lost. It is the wholesale and accelerating destruction of this part of our national heritage which has apparently not yet aroused even the awareness, far less the opposition, of the public. The two salient facts are that hundreds of such buildings which, on practical as well as aesthetic grounds, should be saved, are being torn down all over Scotland today; and that those responsible for this deplorable destruction – as well as those who watch it without making any attempt to arrest it – seem to be utterly careless of the loss to our country and quite ignorant of the potentialities of reconstruction.

The book is in two parts: the first, a review of the advantages of reconstruction as a local and national policy; the second, a discussion of the technique of reconstruction with some typical examples by way of illustration. The second part (which forms the bulk of the book) underlines one of the main contentions of the first – that reconstruction is neither the impractical nor the uneconomic undertaking it is commonly alleged to be. At the same time it provides something in the shape of a manual for anyone embarking upon a reconstruction. While we maintain that the national problem is so acute and so large that only prompt and vigorous public action can provide a solution before it is too late, we believe that the private initiative of men and women of goodwill is just as urgently required. The book is intended for both local authorities and private persons, though for simplicity we have adopted a form of address as to a prospective owner-occupier.

The whole is an attempt to create an awareness of the irreparable harm that is being done, and to show how feasible and desirable from every point of view is the alternative – to preserve all that is still left to us of our traditional little houses and cottages, by bringing them back to life as dwellings which fulfil modern housing requirements. Without them the Scottish scene will suffer a fundamental loss of character and individuality – a loss from which it can never recover.

ACKNOWLEDGMENTS

We gratefully acknowledge our indebtedness to the National Trust for Scotland and the Saltire Society, who have sponsored this book. We also thank Honor McCrindle, George S. Burrows, Frank and Mary Tindall, Michael Crichton-Stuart, and Ian G. Lindsay & Partners, for help in preparing the case histories of houses at Kippen, Dirleton, Haddington, and Falkland; and Alastair Buchanan, H. Anthony Wheeler, Annan of Glasgow, *The Glasgow Herald*, *The Evening Dispatch* of Edinburgh, and Raphael Tuck Ltd., who have supplied photographs for the Plates.

Contents

*   *   *

PHOTOGRAPHIC PLATES

TEXT ILLUSTRATIONS

Drawn by Stuart Harris

I

A Policy of Reconstruction

To appreciate fully the advantages of reconstructing old buildings, both as a national policy and as an individual investment, the effect of present policy must be summarised, and the cause briefly examined. The summary is simple. In Scotland today indiscriminate destruction is proceeding at a rate which will, in the course of the next quarter century, remove from the Scottish scene practically all of the pleasant stone-built cottages and small houses (dating mostly from the eighteenth century) which once graced our country roads and village streets. This vanishing-point is undoubtedly more imminent in Scotland than in any other country in Western Europe – indeed in most of those countries a generally accepted policy of preservation guarantees the survival of a large proportion of such humble but nevertheless important buildings. Scotland is singularly unenlightened in dealing with its old buildings: and furthermore it has fewer, particularly of the humbler sort, than most western countries, because its poverty was such that up to the beginning of the eighteenth century the labouring classes lived in hovels too rudely constructed to survive to the present day. This puts her in the unique position of making greater inroads on a smaller reserve than any of her European neighbours.

This unhappy state of affairs undoubtedly springs from two historical causes. Firstly there was the decline of national consciousness which resulted from the Union of the Parliaments in 1707. Although that measure was extremely unpopular with the generation of Scots which witnessed it, with succeeding generations it took ever-increasing effect in lowering the prestige of all things Scottish and heightening that of anything which showed English influence. By the middle of the nineteenth century that re-orientation of the Scottish mind had become a paramount trend in our national life, at least among the people who were able to produce the most marked effect on it by reason of social position and wealth. Their children were sent to English schools, and to speak Scots became a mark of working-class origin, or at best of eccentricity. Even in Scottish schools our national history and literature were given scant attention. Englishness became a class distinction, and middle-class Scots wishing to better themselves sedulously cultivated it, in some cases even going over to the Episcopal Church which they were careful to call, inaccurately but revealingly, the English Church. The effect on native institutions of all kinds was disastrous: to say of anything that it was Scotch (except whisky, oatmeal, and shortbread) was to imply that it was inferior – of humble, inconsiderable origin. So any building which exhibited good native characteristics was disregarded. (There was one marked exception to this – the vogue for Scottish baronial architecture which followed Queen Victoria's castellated essay at Balmoral. But as Balmorality had its origin in superficial romanticism, expressed in the misapplication of features no longer serving the purpose for which they were conceived – medieval fortification, for example – it cannot be said to have had any real influence on the true appreciation of Scottish buildings.) So strong was the urge to ape the English that by the turn of the century villa residences were being built in Scotland with imitation half-timbered gables, copying a deplorable English fashion for mock-Tudor building – surely one of the most ludicrous examples of slavish imitation. Brick became fashionable because it was English (literally so, for most of it had to be brought from England because of the poor quality of Scottish brick). As the use of stone declined, it became more expensive, and an economic progression of dwindling output and increasing cost was started which has resulted today in the near-extinction of the stone-mason's craft.

In recent years there has been a general revival of national consciousness in Scotland, but so far it has had little effect in arousing public interest in our building tradition. To understand why our stone and lime has been virtually overlooked in this revival, we must consider a second historical cause, which affected not only Scotland, but the whole of Britain. In his book *Our Building Heritage*, W. H. Godfrey, Chairman of the National Buildings Record, writes: 'When Roman civilisation broke before the tide of barbarian invasion the arts were lost, and among them architecture and the technique of building fell into decay . . . The lapse that occurred in the early nineteenth century cannot be described as an entire loss of building technique, but it represented almost as great a break in structural development and building usage as occurred in the Dark Ages. It was not a migration of a barbarous race, but a flood, equally irresistible, of alien purpose that submerged and killed an art that had flourished for centuries. It was not a sudden failing of the science of construction, but a dementia, as rapid in its effect, that turned skill into a blind alley and made invention a mockery.' Mr Godfrey's book is concerned with English building, but that estimate of the effect of the Industrial Revolution applies to an even greater extent in our country. Its disruptive influence, bad enough in all conscience for the architectural seemliness of England, was disastrous in Scotland, where the thread of tradition had already been pitifully weakened by more than a century of increasing political, economic, and cultural subservience. To Scotsmen-on-the-make the fact that a building was traditional in design, and of a respectable age, were twin reasons why it should be destroyed. Such a complete severance of our building tradition explains why the present increasing awareness of national identity among Scots as a whole has so far not included any marked revival of interest in Scottish architecture. In every other facet of our national consciousness there has lingered, through more than two centuries, a faint spark which has lately been fanned to a modest glow. But where buildings are concerned the spark failed to survive the second smothering of the Industrial Revolution.

That is the historical background which to some extent explains (though it cannot possibly justify) the deplorable disregard of old buildings in Scotland today. It has produced an attitude of mind towards them which can best be delineated by enumerating the excuses, one or more of which are commonly advanced to justify the demolition of an old building:

1. *That it contains no sanitary conveniences.* The simple remedy of putting them in, precisely as they are put into a new house, is tacitly ignored. 2. *That the walls are damp.* It is perhaps more understandable that to those ignorant of building technique this should appear a fatal defect, but not that they should simply brush aside constantly reiterated professional assurance that there is seldom any serious difficulty in overcoming this defect. 3. *That the building fails to comply with present-day housing regulations.* The evidence of many reconstructions in which, by the exercise of a little ingenuity, all requirements of regulations in respect of daylighting, ventilation and so on have been met without making the reconstruction uneconomic is completely overlooked. So is the fact that the Department of Health for Scotland, which framed the model by-laws now adopted by the majority of local authorities, specifically recommends that they should be interpreted with intelligent latitude in the exceptional case where serious difficulty may be involved in meeting them to the letter. 4. *That the building impedes traffic* – an excuse usually based on the fallacy that street-widening is *ipso facto* an improvement, whereas there are many examples which prove that a town with narrow streets tends to enjoy a greater degree of immunity from fatal accidents than a town with wide streets. Anything which, within reason, reduces the speed of mechanically-propelled vehicles in town or village

PLATE I

'The grossest single act of vandalism'

THE OLD COLLEGE, GLASGOW: The seventeenth-century College . . . and, from the same spot, the twentieth century's substitute for it.

PLATE 2.

THE TOWN HOUSE AND SANDHAVEN TENEMENTS, CULROSS

A group restored by the Local Authority and by the National Trust for Scotland.

streets reduces the danger to pedestrians. As soon as the streets are widened and bottlenecks removed, allowing traffic to flow faster, serious accidents (as opposed to the minor bumping and scraping common in narrow streets) increase, and as often as not an obstruction (roundabout, pedestrian crossing or island) has to be reintroduced to slow down the flow again. 5. *That people prefer new houses* because they are more comfortable to live in than old houses. Such evidence as is proffered in support of this contention is based on a comparison between new houses and old ones which have not been modernised. But the exact opposite is the experience of Denny Town Council, one of the few local authorities in Scotland to buy and recondition old buildings for municipal housing: it has found that the majority of council tenants ask for reconditioned stone houses in preference to new brick ones. 6. The simplest of all – *that old buildings are ugly.* In this the advocates of demolition set themselves up as arbiters of taste in flat opposition to the consensus of opinion among all people of visual sensitivity, and trained in the arts. Time and again since the end of the second World War have the architects employed by the Department of Health and the Ministry of Works recommended the preservation of threatened buildings because they are of architectural merit, only to meet a blunt contradiction from the local authority – a reiteration, quite unaffected by reasoned argument, that the buildings are ugly and must be pulled down. In 1955 Banff provided a notable instance of such uncompromising independence. On being informed that of a large number of houses which the Town Council had announced its intention to demolish, practically every one was listed by the Department of Health as being eminently worthy of preservation on architectural and historical grounds, the Council approved the statement of its spokesman (as reported in the press) that demolition 'would go merrily on'.

Such are the commonly-advanced excuses for demolition – and 'excuses' is the word rather than 'reasons', because in the

B

great majority of cases the decision to demolish has no logical basis but springs from an unreasoning and prejudiced attitude – at best unsympathetic, at worst animatedly hostile – and any pretence of logic is tacked on afterwards. In contrast, we submit that the case against this policy of destruction (it is no less than a policy) rests on sound reasoning from attested fact, and that for a variety of reasons, some severely practical and some aesthetic, the destruction can be shown to be utterly disastrous for Scotland.

The first practical reason is that the great majority of old buildings of the class we are concerned with in this book (not, that is, of such architectural or historical importance that strict antiquarian restoration is required) are capable of being brought up to modern housing standards at a cost which compares well, and often more than well, with the cost of new building. Such reconstruction turns a liability into an asset. A building to be demolished is normally a liability – the cost of taking it down will far exceed any small value of salvaged material. But if the building is reconstructed, every piece of old work which is sound and usefully retained acquires value in so far as it reduces the new work required. This accession of value can be spectacular. To take an actual example: a pair of derelict condemned cottages in Stirlingshire was bought for £100. Had they been demolished they would have been dear at the price, but when reconstructed it was found that the old work retained (in no respect inferior to new work, and of course adding incomparably more to the character of the whole) represented close on £1000 saved as compared with a new house of equal size. The original buildings were not architectural monuments and could therefore be adapted to suit present-day needs with considerable freedom. The technical problems of bringing such buildings up to modern housing standards are not usually formidable, despite what people who have never tried it assert. It would be, in fact, a quite exceptional case which presented insuperable, or even excessively costly difficulties in making an old house suit our pattern of living and present-day requirements in service and convenience: indeed a properly reconstructed house is often better than a new one of comparable price. With its strapped and plastered walls it is better insulated than the modern house of common eleven-inch cavity wall construction, keeping it warmer in winter and cooler in summer. The same thick walls are responsible for the characteristic splayed window openings which, with proper decorative treatment, create a quality of daylighting such that the rooms seem better lit than many modern rooms with bigger windows. Stone is one of the few building materials that tends to improve in appearance with weathering, and in the Scottish climate is the most satisfactory material for house-building. But today, when quality is regarded as being of secondary importance to cheapness and ease of erection, stone building is passed over because it is more costly than brick and requires more skill and care. And those regrettable reasons for not building new houses in stone have somehow been extended, with no semblance of reason, to justify the wholesale destruction of existing stone houses.

The second practical reason that should condemn this destruction is that our older buildings, be they castles or cottages, are an integral part of the Scottish scene. We have a large tourist industry, and our traditional buildings, just as much as our glens and bens, are part of our stock in this lucrative trade. Stone is the indigenous Scottish building material, but the near cessation of stone building since the first World War has inevitably and decisively cut off the new work from the old. (In most of England, where brick, the common present-day material, has been in use for centuries, the division between new and old is often less marked.) Until the new materials are assimilated into the Scottish tradition it is inevitable that practically any new building, however fine, will be extra-national, and will contribute to the de-Scotticising of the Scottish scene. While we do not suggest that modern building, if it is good, will actually repel tourists, it is true to say that the prevalent low standard of taste is not allowing good design to develop freely, and that the higher cost of even common materials, such as brick and timber, tends to depress the quality of new building in Scotland, class for class, as compared with England and other countries. Is it conceivable that overseas visitors, avid for the sight of evidence of age and tradition in what many of them call the Old Country, are going to wander, entranced, through the avenues and terraces of a typical Scottish council housing scheme or bungaloid colony, as they would through the gaits and wynds of an old village or burgh? The stones of our old buildings are the very fabric of our history, worn and scored by the passing tides of humanity which have lapped against them for generations. An unpretentious cottage with the date 1700 carved on the marriage lintel above the door may have actually seen Prince Charles Edward's army marching south on its way to Derby, and our overseas visitors will note the date, admire the cottage, and probably photograph it, though inside there may be central heating, water laid on in the bedrooms, and a kitchen worthy of an advertisement in the glossiest of magazines. These stone walls are what our visitors have travelled across half the world to see, and every time one is knocked down, our tourist attraction is reduced. We can quote an actual example: a family of Scottish descent from South Africa, who had intended to spend in Scotland five out of six months' leave, were so disappointed by our lack of old buildings, and so shocked by the evidence of our lack of concern for what little remains to us, that after two months they went back to England to explore more fully the many attractive villages and towns they had seen on their way north from London. That change of plan represented a loss of some hundreds of pounds to Scots hoteliers, shopkeepers, and garage proprietors, and is some indication of the increasing harm their businesses will suffer as more and more of our stone and lime is swept away to make room for the standardised and generally characterless brick and cement that grossly mars so much of the Scottish scene today.

To those purely practical and economic reasons that should make us determined to preserve rather than destroy what remains of old building in Scotland, two equally cogent aesthetic reasons must be added. The first is that the general standard of design and craftsmanship in our old houses is incomparably better than that in the vast majority of our houses built in the present century. In other words, we have singularly failed, so far, to profit by the example of our old builders. In their time there was a tradition of building sufficiently integral and strong to ensure that even humble work was of good design. Our country enjoyed a habit of honest craftsmanship and a climate of enlightened taste – indeed, reflecting on the history of the arts, it seems that such a state of affairs had been normal for several centuries until roughly a hundred years ago. Most of our old houses were of the ordinary common run of the work of their time. Sober in the main (though touched occasionally by fancy) they are distinguished by the firm discipline of a good tradition, by a generally consistent standard of craftsmanship, by unforced simplicity and an easy assurance of style. Can anything similar be said of the ordinary common run of house-building today? The period between the two World Wars produced very little of any distinction, and a great deal of degenerate ugliness: of post-war building the most that can be said is that with few honourable exceptions it has not risen above the mediocre. The healthy sense of good design and fitting workmanship which seems to have been normal in the centuries before the Industrial Revolution has not yet returned in strength to stop the outpouring of bad and undisciplined design and poor workmanship. In other fields of industry it may be claimed that mechanisation has created, in place of the traditional handcraft, a new technique of engineering craftsmanship of a generally high standard, but that is certainly not yet true of the building industry, which is in fact one of the most haphazard, with wide variations of efficiency within it. The preservation of our old buildings is therefore not a matter of backward-looking antiquarianism, still less of sentiment: purged of the result of years of neglect, improved where they fall short of modern living standards, spick and span and re-engaged in the everyday traffic of life, they are critics of, and influences on, our present and future standards of building. It is no accident that the most forward-looking architects and planners are amongst the most vigorous advocates of preservation. As Basil Spence, one of the best-known and most modern of our Scottish architects has written: 'How can our young architects of today face the challenge of the future if all evidence of the past is to be destroyed?' We must not despair of our architecture of today and tomorrow, but we cannot shut our eyes to the fact that it has not yet found that sureness of touch, fitness and mannerliness with which even the humblest of our old buildings are instinct. To accustom the younger generation, and generations yet unborn, to the present-day norm in house design and building, by sweeping away all evidence of something better embodied in our old houses, is to debase their sense of values, and make them less satisfactory citizens, whether they be architects, bank clerks, or factory workers. To create a society (as we are in a fair way to doing) which accepts the meretricious tastelessness of the typical bungalow, or the arid bleakness of the average council estate, as normal and even desirable, is to kill all hope for the future. If every old building that exhibits good design and workmanship is to be obliterated, we cannot expect that public opinion will ever demand something better than indifferent design and shoddy execution.

The second aesthetic reason is that a nation must be conscious of its past, its traditions, its history, if it is to continue and develop – to have a future. And how can a people be kept aware of its past if the visible and tangible signs of it are destroyed? It is surely obvious that a child brought up in a burgh or village where there is ample witness to the past in stone and lime is likely to have a much deeper sense of social continuity – of being part of a mature, yet still developing community – than a child brought up in a typical housing scheme, raw, rootless, and lacking any individuality. Good architecture is characterised by having its roots in a region, even when, through very greatness, it transcends regionalism. It is the mark of a virile tradition that it is able to absorb foreign elements and assimilate supranational trends without surrendering its own distinctive character, and Scottish architecture has done this more often and more successfully than almost any other. French, Flemish, German, Scandinavian, English, and Italian importations have been, at many times and in many ways, absorbed into our building tradition, but always without submerging the essentially Scottish character of the work – always, that is, until the great landslide of the nineteenth century. New architecture in Scotland (what there is of it) is not yet the new architecture of Scotland: until it is engrafted into the Scottish mind and spirit it will not mature. But the national tradition embodied in an old building is alive, to enrich, expand, and deepen our understanding of our people and our land. If we in Scotland are to continue to make our distinctive contribution as a nation to the sum of human well-being – surely the object of internationalism as opposed to aggressive nationalism – then we must maintain our national identity, individuality, and tradition. For that it is essential that we shall preserve the buildings which are evidence of our past just as important as the documents so carefully preserved in the Register House in Edinburgh: they should be the yardstick for our present, the inspiration for our future.

These arguments converge on the point that a policy of preservation is a vital part of a grander design for the future good of our country. The prevalent resistance to preservation is in fact but one aspect of a larger failure to match the great task of developing Scotland with the vision, sensitivity, and determination which it demands.' Increasingly it is apparent that our local and national plans for ordered development are in peril of being frustrated, not by economic stringency (serious though that may be) but by this very inability to focus the ultimate and truly essential objectives. One of these objectives must be to keep the country, through all its development, in an organic unity with its past. This is not a nostalgic nor a romantic notion, nor an unprogressive one. It is a simple recognition of the natural process of the growth of a community. As in communities, so in buildings: the old and the new are indissolubly linked together, and the only kind of thinking which will produce a satisfactory development is a thinking which is able to comprehend both old and new and to value them as one. Patrick Geddes, the Scottish father of the whole science of town and regional planning, put this point of organic growth and comprehensive approach at the very heart of his teaching – yet such is the superficiality of commonly accepted notions of town planning that its sacred name is often freely invoked in defence of the very kind of destruction and unintegrated thought he so roundly condemned.

Preservation must not be conceived as a kind of petrifaction – the indefinite fixing of a dead past. It should be conceived as the integration of the past into the present and the future in a living and meaningful way. To restore a fine building while allowing its setting to be so mutilated that it is left in unhappy isolation is to make a mockery of restoration. The same shortsightedness allows a town to be engulfed in a sea of indifferent housing and cheap commercial building even while its citizens are pluming themselves on their preservation of certain fine central areas. The genius of a locality resides in the whole of it, not only in its finest elements. Hence the tragedy of many a street in Scotland, where the loss of a few simple buildings has meant the loss of nearly all that made it itself. Hence the success of comprehensive schemes of restoration – such as at

Dunkeld, Culross, and Falkland, or the group round the Canongate Church in Edinburgh – where fine buildings have been
supported by the restoration of other humbler ones to modern
uses; or at Burntisland, where the old and the patently new
have been integrated in one scheme.

The extent of the wholesale substitution of bad buildings for
good ones which began with the Industrial Revolution and
continues unabated today, and the tremendous loss which
Scotland has suffered and continues to suffer, can be sufficiently
illustrated by four examples.

In 1727 Daniel Defoe, author of *Robinson Crusoe*, published
an account of a tour through Scotland. He was greatly im-
pressed by Glasgow, and particularly its architecture. 'It is a
large, stately, and well-built city . . . and the four principal
streets are the fairest for breadth, and the finest built that I
have ever seen in one city together. The houses are all of stone,
and generally uniform in height, as well as in front. The lower
stories, for the most part, stand on vast Doric columns, with
arches, which open into the shops, adding to the strength as
well as the beauty of the building. In a word, 'tis one of the
cleanliest, most beautiful, and best-built cities in Great Britain.'
Today, of all the domestic buildings which so aroused his admiration – an Englishman's admiration for a highly distinctive
national style which was evidently quite unfamiliar to him,
and which he might well, therefore, have disliked – there is
only *one solitary survival*, Provand's Lordship, a fifteenth-century
cathedral manse, now preserved as a museum and clubroom
by an antiquarian society. The obliteration of the old town
involved the grossest single act of vandalism in our whole
national history – the destruction of the old university, the
finest range of medieval buildings in Scotland, to make room
for a railway goods yard, which is already scheduled for removal.

In Stirling, once a town to rival Edinburgh in its profusion of
admirable town houses dating from the sixteenth century, and

with equally strong historic associations, the whole of the old town was allowed to fall into decay such that overseas and English visitors assumed that it had been blitzed during the war. Only by means of a determined newspaper campaign, and the united and dogged pertinacity of the National Trust for Scotland, the Ancient Monuments Commission, the Historic Buildings Council, and the Department of Health for Scotland, reinforced by the most generous financial grants, was the Town Council induced to undertake the restoration of half a dozen houses. Of the old town, which could have been an unrivalled tourist attraction and a delightful place in which to live, not more than a score of houses remain: and while some of the new buildings in it are in keeping with their old surroundings, others are ordinary council houses which no local authority with any sense of responsibility for its unique architectural heritage could have allowed to be built on such a site.

In Perth, once the capital of Scotland, and described by Sir Walter Scott as the Fair City, practically all the medieval buildings have been destroyed and the eighteenth-century frontages of the principal streets wantonly broken to make room for petrol stations (in the principal city streets!), and office blocks and cheap stores. A town council with any real regard for architectural amenity would have insisted that the pleasant and dignified street frontages at least be kept intact.

In the old town of Edinburgh mass destruction occurred in the second half of the nineteenth century, when much of the medieval building was swept away in what was euphemistically known as the City Improvement Scheme. But fortunately the old town was too large to make a clean sweep economically possible, and while most of the very best buildings – churches as well as houses – were destroyed, a good many were left to disintegrate gradually during the ensuing century. Isolated buildings were restored in the 1930's and a comprehensive plan for the restoration of the whole area was made and adopted at the end of the last war. Rebuilding is now at last proceeding on a considerable scale, but the city is paying the penalty of long neglect in that many buildings which might once have been saved are now considered to be past redemption.

These four examples typify the damage that has been done to every burgh and village in Scotland. Though today there is undoubtedly a belated stirring of concern about the fate of our building heritage, it is unfortunately offset by the greatly increased speed of destruction. Methods used to flatten air-fields during the war are now used to flatten old buildings, and a whole row of houses may be obliterated in a day. Bulldozing has great advantages in the eyes of local authorities – it gets the buildings down too quickly for effective protest to be organised, and it reduces the possibility of anything being discovered in the course of demolition that might delay it. This method was most effectively used in the recent clearances in the old town of Stirling: no one will ever know what carved stones or plaster work were momentarily revealed for the last time as the mechanical excavator scooped up walls that had reflected four hundred years of Scotland's story.

To lay on local authorities the chief blame for the irreparable damage being done to our building heritage and to the Scottish scene, urban and rural, is not to suggest that they are the only destructive agency; but that in our social organisation today they bear wider responsibilities and wield greater powers than all the other destroyers put together. Nor is it to suggest that they are singular in their attitude to old buildings: in this they are not only the representatives, but truly representative of the mass of their constituents. The prevalent torpor of imagination and the unthinking opinion that equates new construction with progress and reconstruction with reaction, are shared by the majority of councillors; and in the crowded agenda of council business there is little time to establish the case for preservation or to give the individual thought which each restoration requires. Lack of vision and pressure of work combine to erect standardisation of building into a doctrine, and since restoration is incapable of standardisation it becomes an aberration meriting either apathy or, in many documented cases, active hostility. Yet the decision for or against preservation is almost entirely in the hands of these authorities, and their statutory powers are such that, if they were exerted, vandalism would be stopped tomorrow, and schemes of restoration both public and private could be set on foot. It is not the power that is lacking, but the will to apply it. If local authorities having these powers, and having a prime duty to further the best interests of the community, are determined to take the easy way out and use old buildings only as a source of road-bottoming in new housing estates, how can they escape blame?

The attitude of more enlightened town councils in England makes an interesting contrast. In Chester the Council bought one entire side of a street to prevent the imminent intrusion of a multiple store building in a hitherto unbroken seventeenth-century street frontage: in Bath the Council put preservation orders on a thousand houses at once. These councils realise that the maintenance of the character of their city is essential to its future. Look at York, Norwich, Canterbury – and then look at any equivalent Scottish town. The comparison is nothing short of tragic.

Yet even in England such enlightenment in local authorities is the exception rather than the rule. Again we quote W. H. Godfrey, and again we emphasise that everything he has to say about the present situation in England applies to a much more marked degree in Scotland, where no local authority can yet be described as truly enlightened in its attitude to old buildings. 'With a full sense of responsibility for what I say it seems to me that the chief enemies of the English scene, as it is known and loved by all who have eyes to see, and the bar to its orderly development and equipment to meet the rightful needs of today, have been among those entrusted with the task of improving the health and housing conditions of the people. In their new schemes they are often handicapped by the need of a rigid economy – a condition certainly not conducive to good building – but they have a greater disability in their ignorance of structural technique in the buildings they condemn. Medical officers of health who would be ashamed to make gross errors in the diagnosis of disease, fail to diagnose the condition of a building through complete unacquaintance with its organic structure. And not doctors alone but a large proportion of practising architects are so unfamiliar with traditional construction that they are misled into reading a mortal malady when the trouble is nothing more than a superficial lack of condition. These erroneous judgments are welcomed and encouraged by local authorities whose members are too often guided entirely by the prejudices that have been in vogue for three generations. The modern conveniences in a house are the only things that interest them, and their imagination cannot grasp the potentialities of reconditioning and re-equipment. . . . It is this ignorance and this prejudice that must be fought if we are not to slip into sheer retrogression.'

The fight is waged stubbornly in Scotland by a few bodies, voluntary and official, but most evidence of success is more apparent than real. Thanks to their efforts, and in particular to the bulldog tenacity of their fights to save specific buildings, there is undoubtedly a growing minority among the public who deplore the destruction, but they are still too few to exert any decisive influence on public opinion. Many local authorities now profess to favour preservation, but all too often their actions in particular cases prove this to be mere lip-service and show that there has been no change of heart – that ignorance is as deep and prejudice as strong as ever. The battles to save threatened buildings, now practically continuous, are essentially rearguard actions – trying to delay demolition, to rouse public concern, to encourage private initiative. Gravely handicapped by lack of funds and powers, the bodies concerned are only occasionally successful in their championing, and when to that is added the fact that their resources will allow them to intervene only when the building is of exceptional importance or the demolition of exceptional wantonness, it will be seen that the sum of their success, in point of quantity, is minute in relation to the total volume of demolition going on. To say that is not to disparage their valiant efforts, but to state the plain fact that the odds against them make the fight hopeless unless they receive some massive access of power.

One of many deplorable features of the situation is that planning control to prevent the continued destruction of old buildings in Scotland has been in force (if one can so describe it) ever since the end of the war, but has proved in practice to be nothing more than a broken reed. Indeed it is no exaggeration to say that it has proved worse than useless, because it gives an entirely illusory appearance of being a safeguard. On the Department of Health for Scotland was laid a statutory duty to prepare lists of buildings, not already protected under the Ancient Monuments Act, which should be preserved because of their architectural or historical value. Architects with particular knowledge of the Scottish building tradition have been employed to compile the lists, which are very exhaustive, and no building so listed may be demolished or externally altered without two months' notice to the Department. It was presumably hoped by the originators of the scheme that in the two months' grace the Department of Health would be able to persuade the would-be demolishers, with the aid of generous reconstruction grants, to reconsider their intention. It was a forlorn hope: the Department's pleas, advice, and offers of help have almost without exception been ignored, and at the end of the two months the building has been demolished. The proviso that in cases of particular importance the Secretary of State for Scotland might intervene with a preservation order has never been invoked – of the hundreds of listed buildings which have been turned into road-bottoming since the war, not one has evidently been regarded by a Secretary of State as of sufficient importance to induce him to take what is apparently considered the impolitic step of frustrating the destructive mania which is rampant in Scotland today.

Without any effective Governmental safeguard, and without the pressure of an informed public opinion, the doom of what remains of our building heritage might well seem to be sealed. But the case for preservation is unassailable, and we still have sufficient faith in the good sense of our fellow Scots to believe that the present widespread apathy is the result of ignorance rather than a positive wish to see the last remains of an essential part of the Scottish tradition and way of life irrevocably destroyed.

That faith we have embodied in this book, which combines an appeal to reason with a detailed study of the practical aspects of reconstruction, and is, we believe, the first to deal with the problem in Scotland. That many books have been published which deal in a similar way with the English building tradition encourages us to think that they may be partly responsible for the fact that the situation is much less desperate there.

We offer the book to all Scots who care about our country's past and future (which are but two aspects of the same thing) in the earnest hope that, despite any shortcomings, it may convince them of the clamant need for a general policy of restoration, and help them to translate that conviction into action.

2

A Manual of Practical Notes

1. The Approach to the Work

Before discussing in detail the methods and techniques involved in reconditioning an old building there are certain general principles which must be enunciated. A reconditioning or reconstruction project not only differs physically in almost every respect from a new building project, but it also requires a quite distinct attitude of mind in the prospective occupiers, the architect, and even, if to a lesser extent, the tradesmen. It involves – and this is a fundamental factor which must be accepted – a certain limitation of freedom, a willingness to compromise here and there and to submit to some measure of dictation by the old building itself. You (and as already said, we have adopted the convention that we are addressing a prospective owner-occupier, though let that not deter other readers) cannot envisage your ideal home and then try to impose it in detail on an existing building – or if you do the result is practically certain to be unsatisfactory from every point of view. To make a success of a reconstruction you must have the proper approach to the project.

The purpose of reconditioning an old building should be to give it a new lease of life in its own right – to restore it to useful service in as nearly as reasonably possible the form and outward appearance in which it was originally built. That does not preclude converting, say, an old watermill into a house, but it does impose on the converter an obligation not to disguise unnecessarily the original purpose of the building. A good conversion preserves, as far as possible, the character of

PLATE 3.   MENSTRIE CASTLE, CLACKMANNANSHIRE

Restored by the Local Authority, with the aid of the
Historic Buildings Council for Scotland, the Pilgrim
Trust, and public subscriptions in Scotland and Nova
Scotia (whose founder, Sir William Alexander, was
born here). The castle, converted into flats, is now
the dominant and distinctive feature of a new housing
estate.

PLATE 4.   CATHEDRAL STREET, DUNKELD

Part of the comprehensive restoration of the old town and the
approaches to the Cathedral, which is being carried out by the
National Trust for Scotland and the Local Authority.

the original – indeed that should be one of the objects. To take four existing walls and make them the nucleus of a modern villa, a garage or a chip shop, is destruction, not conversion.

The attitude of mind, then, must be completely sympathetic to the old building: it must also embrace courage, cautious optimism, and vision. Courage there must be, because re-conditioning is inevitably a journey into the unknown. This is a point we shall make twenty times, but it needs frequent repetition – that it is always difficult and often impossible to assess accurately from a survey what work (and therefore cost) will be entailed. The journey will have a happy ending – of that there need be no doubt. But to undertake at all a journey on which unforeseen difficulties and expenses are quite likely to be met – that does require a certain amount of courage. Optimism is equally necessary, if only because prophets of doom will creep from every corner as soon as your intention is known, foretelling a hopeless struggle against dry rot and every other ill a house is heir to. An impervious surface of optimism is your best protection. But let it be tempered with caution – with the realisation that hidden defects may be revealed in the course of the work and also that it may prove impossible to carry out the reconstruction exactly as you had envisaged it. And lastly, vision – perhaps the most important of all, for without it the people perish, and good houses are destroyed. It takes vision to see through even the most superficial dirt, dilapidation, and decay. If some of the windows are smashed: if rainwater from a broken gutter or choked down-pipe has stained the walls: if there is some broken harling outside and some broken plaster inside: if squatters, or even children, have left a litter of rubbish, rags and filth – then ninety-nine people out of a hundred will solemnly assure you that the building is ruinous beyond redemption. Yet all those symptoms of neglect – they are nothing more – could be put right, in a small house in other respects up to modern habitation standards, for a hundred pounds or so. Even the elementary vision to see that

c

is curiously rare. But your vision must be rather more penetrating: as well as seeing through such superficial lack of condition, you must be able to see beyond the existing internal
plan of the building, and visualise its possibilities if the plan
were altered to some extent – if a partition were demolished
here, a new door opening made there.

Assuming, then, that you have the proper attitude of mind,
you take the first practical step – finding the building. Here
you have a choice of two roads, and should probably explore
both. You can look for an old house which is still in habitable
condition, but which you intend to improve, or you can look
for a more or less derelict building which you will recondition.
Obviously the first will entail a very much larger initial outlay,
but much less subsequent expense. Such a house can be found
sooner or later through the normal channels of property agents
and newspaper advertisements. But those channels will be
of no use in a search for a derelict building, for no owner is
going to spend money in trying to sell something that has
practically no commercial value. You will have to find such a
building for yourself, and the obvious way is to go into the
highways and by-ways and look for it. Two or three explora-
tory expeditions in the chosen areas should be sufficient, because Scotland is littered with buildings which have been
allowed to fall into decay. Having found it, you want to find
the owner: neighbouring occupiers can probably give some
information, but if not, try the police or the valuation roll.
Your approach to the owner, when found, should be cautious.
You will probably be told: 'It's condemned,' as if that closed
the matter, for the average owner believes a closing order to be
irrevocable. Your continued interest may arouse suspicion
and the safer approach is to show more interest in the site. But
if the owner shows any tenderness for the existing building,
then you can safely be frank, and try to enlist his or her sympathy in your aim.

At this stage, as indeed at every stage in a reconstruction, be prepared for set-backs. A succession of owners may flatly refuse to have any dealings with you, or, while not refusing, may put an obviously inflated value on the property: generally speaking you should not consider paying much more than £100 for a condemned cottage or small house. But having found an owner willing, on reasonable terms, to transfer a suitable property to you, and having secured agreement in principle (it must be no more as yet), you should make your own pre-preliminary survey of the building. This is not a substitute for a professional survey, which is absolutely essential before you sign on any dotted line. We merely suggest that you should try to save yourself the needless expense of bringing an architect on a wild goose chase: that you should satisfy yourself, by a very rough assessment, that there is at least a possibility that the building is suited to your purse and purpose. You have presumably made up your mind how much you can afford to spend. Say, for argument's sake, that it is in the region of £1000. For that sum you cannot possibly undertake the reconditioning of a building which requires any major repairs or alterations. You will, in fact, have to find a building which is only derelict in the technical sense that it may not be occupied as a dwelling house until it has been brought up to modern housing standards. That will probably entail damp-proofing at ground-floor level and providing adequate sanitation, hot water system, and perhaps some increase in the window area. That work, with minor repairs necessitated by previous neglect, is likely to take every penny of your £1000, unless you happen to be a tradesman and can do some of the work yourself. But assuming you have no talent, beyond perhaps painting, you must accept the fact that with £1000 to spend you are wasting money if you ask an architect to survey a building in which, for example, part of the roof has fallen in. With that financial limit you can only usefully consider a building that appears to be structurally sound, in which water supply and drainage are not going to be a great expense, and in which you can accept the existing internal planning without much alteration.

To take another hypothetical round figure, if you can afford to spend about £2000, you can obviously tackle a much more extensive reconstruction. In that case you are justified in having a professional survey made even though the walls and roof are obviously in need of considerable repair, although drainage seems inadequate and the existing plan is unsuited to your needs.

All that may appear very obvious, but it is offered as a warning against unrealistic optimism. Many people, possibly with vague recollections of hearing how a friend of a friend made a sweet little house out of a couple of cottages in Kent for a few hundred pounds in the 1930's imagine that the same sort of thing can be done today. But labour and materials cost more than three times as much as they did then, and regulations have become far more exacting. A few hundred pounds today will be required for sanitation and a hot water system alone. And remember, too, that no building society is likely to be prepared to advance money for the reconditioning of derelict property.

Having made your own amateur survey, and decided that there is at least an apparent possibility that the building could be reconditioned at a cost within your means, your next move is to employ an architect to make the preliminary survey. You may be advised to ask the local builder and contractor either to make the survey, or to give an opinion before you decide to consult an architect. Ignore the advice. We would be the last to deny that there are many local contractors whose opinion would be valuable, and who would be sympathetic to your project. But you cannot depend on finding such a man, and you may hit on one who lacks the technical knowledge to advise you, or who is completely out of sympathy with your intention. Nor can you count on his advice being disinterested – it is obviously to his advantage to persuade you to scrap the old building and start afresh. We have in mind a certain group of old cottages which were either to be restored or replaced. A contractor roundly condemned their perfectly sound rubble walls as 'just rubbish', and because it came from a 'practical man' that opinion carried such weight with the local authority that it was with extreme difficulty that the cottages were saved and restored. Today they stand as a monument to the unreliability of that 'practical man's' advice. So if you have satisfied yourself that the building is worth surveying, go straight to an architect. He may decide to consult a builder, but he will be better able to judge the worth of the opinion he receives from him.

In the normal course of house purchase the prospective buyer often employs a surveyor to examine the property, but a surveyor is unlikely to be the best person to advise you in this case, because it is far removed from the normal one to which he is accustomed. Also there is an obvious advantage in bringing the architect of your choice, who will be responsible for the work if you decide to go ahead, on to the scene at the earliest possible stage. But we must emphasise that the problem of finding the right architect may well prove just as difficult as finding the right building, and most certainly requires no less care. Not every architect is fitted by temperament or training for the task of reconditioning an old structure. Such work takes up much more of his time than the same amount of new building, and requires a great deal of ingenuity in overcoming many small but stubborn problems. It puts him to a lot of trouble: the time spent in supervision is bound to be heavy, and to the normal duty of exacting a good standard of workmanship is added the task of inspiring contractor and tradesman to take an intelligent interest in work which is far from straightforward. Unless the architect himself has a keen personal interest in this type of work he is unlikely to be successful in it. He must also have an adequate knowledge of the history of design and construction, combined with a lively sympathy for the building in front of him, and a willingness to learn from it. Many, though by no means all, of the younger men have no interest outside modern design, and lack the necessary training and aptitude. On the other hand, it is unfortunate that the training of many older men was infected by the decadent 'tradition' of recent decades, and that their understanding of the real tradition is much less profound than might be supposed: the sort of traditionalism which they may introduce can be just as harmful as the illiterate modernisms to be expected from a young architect with little respect for an old building. Then again, compared to new building, the amount of reconstruction work going on in Scotland is very small, and the architect's opportunity to gain experience in it is correspondingly limited. From all of which you will gather that the choice of architect is not wide, and that you should make careful enquiry before you select one and, if possible, see a reconstruction for which he has been responsible.

Having found him, remember always that he too is making a journey into the unknown. You must not be surprised and disappointed if more than once in the course of the work he has to tell you that some unforeseen difficulty has arisen, some unexpected defect been uncovered. No two old buildings present precisely the same problems, nor are the problems necessarily ascertainable at the outset. There are only general principles applying to such work, and their particular application differs in each individual case. It would be safe to say that an architect with a dozen reconstructions to his credit would be very lucky to complete his thirteenth without meeting, if not a new problem, at least a new variant of a known one. So when he comes on the scene, and tells you whether or not, in his opinion, the building you have chosen can be reconstructed for the money you have to spend, he is making a guess, and the only certainty is that his guess is a great deal better than yours. As he will undoubtedly warn you, there must be considerable latitude allowed for permissible error. It is simply not possible to estimate reconstruction costs with the precision rightly expected in the case of new works, and the estimate must include a far more liberal allowance for unforeseen contingencies.

When you come to decide what is to be done with the building (and indeed throughout the progress of the work) you should bear in mind that the mark of successful reconstruction is a happy marriage between old and new, wherein each gains from the other. If they are at odds, an unsatisfactory, unhappy building is the inevitable result. This harmony will escape you unless you realise that the structure of an old building, however ruinous, is still instinct and alive with the art and craftmanship which made it, and that, whatever the extent of your alterations and adaptations, your essential task is to conserve this vitality as a full partner in the finished work. If you lose sight of this, nothing but sheer luck will stand between you and failure.

This principle underlies the point made earlier, that the appearance and character of the building should never be unnecessarily altered or disguised. You should accept the basic external design, making no more than the minimum of alteration necessary to allow you to transform the interior into a convenient dwelling. You will find almost invariably that strict economy in structural alteration to outside walls goes hand in hand with success in your main purpose. To attempt to convert, say, a pair of old cottages into the semblance of a modern bungalow (we could show you examples, complete with oriel windows) would be to destroy the original cottages as effectively as if they had been demolished – and would probably cost as much as a new building.

Repairs to old work should be treated simply, and kept to a minimum. Superficial damage to surfaces – chipped corners on stonework for example – should be left untouched. They are part and parcel of the character the building has acquired with the passing years, like the lines in an old face, and it will only be harmed by the pock-marks of little niggling repairs.

But damage which threatens the soundness of the structure must obviously be made good. If, in the course of alteration, any sound material has been displaced, use it again if there is an opportunity. In most instances this is an economy, but in the few cases where refurbishing is likely to be slightly more costly than replacement, remember that every piece of visible old work jettisoned represents a certain loss of character in the finished house. For example an original door, even if it requires patching, will almost certainly contribute more to the character of the house than any new door. An obvious extension of this principle is to buy sound second-hand material whenever possible.

Before leaving the general principles which should govern the rehabilitation of old buildings, three special cases must be mentioned. The first is the case of a building with particular architectural features or historical associations. It may not seem likely that such a building will come into the possession of someone who simply wants to reconstruct an old house, but such is the general disregard of old buildings in Scotland that it is by no means impossible. Assuming that you recognise the intrinsic merit of the features, whatever they may be (or that your architect draws your attention to it), you must accept the additional responsibility involved. Take a perfectly possible case: in the course of reconstruction some part of a very ordinary plaster ceiling is taken down, unexpectedly revealing decorated joists of an earlier period. In such a case it is nothing less than your duty to procure expert guidance in the treatment and preservation of the painted ceiling – the National Trust for Scotland will be more than willing to advise you, and if the additional expense involved is a real difficulty, may be able to get you financial help. In other cases the feature may be obvious from the start – fine panelling, a carved stone fireplace, an authenticated instance of Prince-Charlie-slept-here. Each places on the new owner a responsibility not to destroy something which is of a value overriding personal considerations.

You cannot, morally, regard it as something you have bought, to treat as best suits you. Each is a tiny part of our national heritage: you hold it in trust, and to preserve it you should be prepared to modify your plans for reconstruction.

The second special case is of a building which you want to reduce in size. If it proves to be an old building which has been added to, you are probably improving it by removing additions, especially if they are Victorian ones. But if you contemplate removing some part of the original building you are almost certainly going to harm it. In that case we beg you to think again. Discuss with your architect the feasibility of leaving the unwanted part wind and watertight, but otherwise unfinished. You may be glad of the room for expansion in future years, even as storage space, and it may be an asset if you ever want to sell the house. And remember that demolition is costly.

The third case is that of a building which will not be big enough for your purpose without an addition. The obvious advice is to suggest that you start again, and find another building that needs no additions. But supposing that you have valid reasons for saying that no other building could possibly suit you as well, then the character of the original can be the only guide in deciding what form of addition would best become it. There must be harmony between the new and the old. That is not to say that the addition need be a slavish copy or a quasi-traditional compromise: the fake not only obscures the truth but has no soul to call its own, and you do nothing but harm to a virile old building if you tack on to it something which is timid and insipid to the point of dullness. These seemingly safe solutions lead straight to disaster. A much more radical approach is necessary. An old building owes much of its strength and dignity to the fact that it is unselfconsciously of its time and presents a direct, unforced answer to the needs it was built to serve. Anything you add must have its own parallel authenticity, yet marry with the old. The keys

to success in that marriage are three: first, matching of architectural scales; second, good relation of proportions; third,
sensitive handling of materials. (Analyse any ugly extension
of an eighteenth-century building and you will find the root of
its ugliness in the coarse scale characteristic of post-Georgian
building, or ill-assorted proportions, or unhappy clashes of
colour or texture.) These three requirements do not tie the
designer's hands – they can be as well satisfied by straightforward stone building using salvaged materials as by an extension which is frankly – but not brashly – of the twentieth
century. The overriding requirement (of which these three
are but different aspects) is that the original and the addition
must become integral parts of one inclusive whole. Where the
original is already a very definite whole – a unified architectural
form – an addition will only destroy the design. Successful
addition is possible only when the original design is sufficiently
free to tolerate it, and even then you must take the greatest care
to avoid architectural solecisms and to make the enlarged
building a balanced and satisfactory composition.

Returning to the main stream of straightforward reconditioning – in so far as it can ever be described as straightforward – we would close this chapter on a note of warning.
You are very likely to pass through periods of depression in the
course of the work. Unforeseen difficulties, as we have emphasised, may well arise. While it is unlikely that the extra
expense involved will exceed your architect's allowance for
contingencies, they will probably cause delays and frustration,
and unless you are prepared for them you may find your courage
sinking, your faith faltering. Then the faint-heart which is in
all of us may whisper with horrid insistence: 'What possessed
me to embark on this? Why didn't I play safe and sensible
and build a new house in which eventualities could be fore-
seen?' The only answer to that doubting voice is faith, backed
by the knowledge that hundreds of old houses have been reconstructed, and that where the reconstruction has been

properly done, the risk of anything less than complete satisfaction is negligible. In every case of which we have knowledge the final result has come up to expectations – in many cases expectations have been surpassed. The author of the Epistle to the Hebrews has said that 'Faith is the substance of things hoped for', and on the relatively mundane level of the reconstruction of old buildings that is as true as on the spiritual plane of which it was written. We have yet to hear of the substance, in stone and lime, which has not, in the end, justified the faith.

2. Design and Planning

Once you have purchased the building, the architect's first step is to make a thorough survey to ascertain its structural system, its dimensions and levels, its materials, and its defects. On earlier visits possibilities of doing this or that with the building may have suggested themselves, but it is a mistake to allow ideas to crystallise into a definite scheme before the survey proper has given a clear and complete picture of the building as it stands. Without such a picture to work from you are, to say the least, unlikely to devise the best possible plan or to make a sympathetic reconstruction. The design should be developed out of the old building, not imposed upon it, and the first essential is that intimate knowledge of the original which only a thorough survey can give. The initial survey also bears on the building contract and the final cost of works, for although in this type of work you cannot obviate the risk of unforeseen difficulties, an accurate and exhaustive survey reduces that risk to the minimum and spares you much irritating delay, extra works and extra expense. The survey is in fact the first step towards control of contract and cost.

If the building is in fair condition, the survey may well be carried out in one operation, but if it is dilapidated the survey should be divided into two parts: the first a survey of the structural system and the finishings, the second a detailed inspection and measurement done after decayed finishings and obviously redundant features have been taken away and the inner structure exposed. Plaster and woodwork often hide the true extent (or the very existence) of defects, and moreover it is not unusual to find original features – doors, windows, or recesses – which have been covered up by later additions but which may be useful or effective in the new scheme.

Reconstruction jobs may be broadly divided into two types. The first is that in which the bulk of the work as finished is original and the new work limited to general repairs, installation of modern services, and small alterations to individual rooms. Since the old is the dominant part, the new work must follow it in style if not match it precisely, and if the style is sophisticated the new finishings are likely to be expensive. Here preservation and economy walk hand in hand, for the less that is done by way of alteration the less the cost. In the second type of reconstruction – the rehabilitation of a dilapidated building – this equation may not always be true. Although, as we have remarked earlier, the saving of old work will in general mean the saving of money, in particular details it may be cheaper to scrap an old fragment rather than incorporate it in a larger bulk of new work. But that alone should not be allowed to settle the matter. The survey will enable you to analyse the elements of the old building into (1) those which are so badly decayed that they must be replaced, (2) those which are fairly sound and which if repaired will be worth more than the cost of repair, and (3) those which are sound enough to retain and are worth keeping if the cost can be justified on grounds other than financial. This third group is the difficult one, so nice is the balance between the various considerations of preservation, planning convenience, ease of building, and cost. You should not surrender too easily to the short-term consideration of cost, but try always to give proper weight to such long-term factors as the desirability of preservation and the convenience of the plan. You must make an effort to look as far ahead as the completed house and see the immediate problem in that perspective. Old work retained – even a fragment of little or no obvious beauty or importance – can have an effect on the character of the finished job quite disproportionate to its apparent value in the early stages. Quite apart from the cause of preservation for preservation's sake, this long-range result reflects back on the immediate question of cost, for the ultimate valuation of the house depends not on the money sunk in it but on its final state, including its character, and this capital value is the true yardstick for the expenses of the work. More often than not, the restorer's sense of duty to the old building turns out to be his best practical guide.

The more extensive type of reconstruction gives you an opportunity to remodel the interior to suit your convenience; indeed it may be made to fit your needs in much the same way as a new house, though the fixed details of aspect, load-bearing walls, external doors, window openings, and floor levels may make the problem more intricate. Replanning, however radical a departure from the original, can nevertheless make its own contribution to the building as a restoration. The plan determines the shapes and proportions of rooms, which in turn play a major part in creating the character of the building. A plan which reflects the directness and simplicity of the original structure is as necessary to proper restoration as the stones and other parts of the fabric which you have preserved.

In reorganising the plan of a two-storey house (especially if you are changing the uses of rooms and so altering the balance of the accommodation) you may encounter some difficulty at the stairs. The different plans which can be devised to suit the four walls of any house, new or old, are limited in their essential forms to a handful of basic types, each of which has its own characteristic position for the stairs; and the underlying cause of your difficulty may be either that the existing staircase, while basically suitable, is not quite in the ideal position, or that its position is really inconsistent with the new plan. In the first case, your difficulty is not likely to be insuperable though there may be some residual awkwardness in the final plan; but if the cause of the trouble is a radical inconsistency the plan may not work without considerable forcing. If there are gains to weigh against it (such as the saving of a good staircase) some awkwardness will be tolerable and should be accepted, but if the awkwardness is beyond the limit of justifiable inconvenience or if you cannot combine the staircase with what is, all things considered, the only satisfactory plan, you should cut the Gordian knot by altering, transferring, or wholly replacing the stairs. Confused planning is a form of ugliness and should be avoided unless there are compelling reasons to the contrary.

We differ from our forefathers in being keenly aware of the need for sunshine in the main living space of our houses (the living-room, dining-room, and kitchen). For reasons no longer valid (for example, to overlook the main fields of the farm) the rooms in some old houses face away from the sun; and in such cases one of the first objects in replanning will be to obtain sunshine in the right places. In narrow plans it is usually possible to extend the living-room to pass through the house from front to back and in this way to secure a southerly or westerly aspect. If lobbies and stairs are brought to the north or east sides of the house, the rooms will be better placed to receive sunlight. The objection that old windows are often smaller than modern ones is less important than it seems. The value of sunlight in a house lies not so much in its direct therapeutic quality (which is mostly extinguished by its passage through the window-glass) as in its stimulant effect. It follows that the quantity received is less important than the length of time it lasts, and that the sheer size of windows is less important than their placing – for instance, rooms with small windows on each of two sunny walls will in most cases have sunshine longer than rooms lit by big windows on one wall.

In town property the scope of manoeuvre for sunlight is necessarily restricted, but much of the charm of the reconstructed country cottage is due to the extra periods of sunshine caught – one might sometimes say snatched – by quite small windows in side or back walls.

When designing a new house, an architect selects windows of a size to give adequate daylighting to the rooms he has already planned; but in the case of a reconstruction the procedure is reversed, for the windows exist, their area and therefore the amount of daylight they will admit is fixed, and the rooms must be adjusted to fit them. For this reason, daylighting must be studied at a very early stage in planning.

Building by-laws generally prescribe a rough rule of thumb to assess minimum daylighting for a habitable room; namely, that the total glazed area shall not be less than one-tenth of the habitable floor area. Yet the level of daylighting is in reality affected by a whole complex of factors – the shape and size of room and window, the placing of a window and the amount of sky visible through it – and though the rule of thumb may give a fair approximation in the conditions for which it was first devised (that is, in town, where obstruction of the sky by adjacent buildings is normal) it is manifestly unreasonable to apply it with the same strictness to a rural cottage of open outlook where a window will give about twice the light it would give in average town conditions. Satisfactory lighting depends on quality as well as sheer quantity of light. Visual comfort is greatly affected by contrasts and gradations of tone, and by sparkle and glare. Windows of the eighteenth and early nineteenth centuries are models of good design in this respect, and experience shows that they give perfectly satisfactory and agreeable lighting even when their area is barely up to minimum by-law standard. It is as unnecessary as it is ill-judged to spoil an old façade by introducing large picture windows in the current fashion.

In planning for daylight, the obvious strategy is to bring the larger rooms to those walls which have most windows, and to place small rooms, lobbies and cupboards next to the other walls. The glass area may often be enlarged quite simply by glazing or half glazing an external door or by lowering the sill of a window to turn it into a french window. The advantage of forming a living-room with windows on opposite sides has already been mentioned. In upper rooms supplementary roof lighting is a possible but rather undesirable expedient. The question of slapping new windows is considered later. One most useful device for adjusting floor areas to suit the day-lighting standard is the built-in cupboard or wardrobe. The floor area absorbed by such a fitment is not counted as 'habit-able', whereas the floor covered by a movable storage unit of the same kind is taken to be potentially habitable and must be included in computing the floor area.

To ensure adequate ventilation, by-laws lay down a mini-mum height for the ceilings of habitable rooms (at present it is seven feet six inches). Substandard ceiling heights may be increased by a variety of means. When renewing floors or roof ties it is sometimes possible to adjust their levels to gain the few vital inches required. An old ceiling can be removed and a new ceiling formed higher up between the joists. If necessary, the ceiling can be done away with altogether, and the boards of the floor above left exposed; but besides making a possibly undesirable change in the character of the room, this expedient raises serious practical difficulties in getting an acceptable finish, in preventing dust from falling through the joints in the floor above, and in keeping noise transmission down to a reasonable level. Yet with the best will in the world it is not always possible to raise ceilings or to lower floors sufficiently to bring ceiling heights up to standard. Fortunately in such cases authorities are empowered by statute to exercise reasonable latitude in interpreting the regulations, provided they are satisfied that every possible effort to comply has been made, and that the means of through ventilation are adequate.

St Andrew's House (*left*) and Key-House, at the gates
of Falkland Palace.

PLATE 5.   FALKLAND, FIFE
For Case Histories, see p. 138

Moncreif House, opposite the Palace.

SOMERVILLE STREET, BURNTISLAND
Restored by the Local Authority as part of the
redevelopment of a central area of the town.

PLATE 6

SWANSTON, EDINBURGH
A village in the city's green belt, restored in its
entirety by the Local Authority.

Since in England the minimum requirement for ceiling heights in reconstructed houses is seven feet (and even lower heights are permitted in special cases) it is unlikely that Scottish healths will suffer.

New openings are usually expensive, and often cannot be made without upsetting the balance of the elevations. If they cannot be avoided, they should be as few as possible and be worked into the design with the utmost discretion. Apart from reopening blocked-up windows (which are quite common although often concealed under harling) it is virtually impossible to form a new opening in a regular and complete elevation without ruining it. More can be done with the irregular and informal elevation, yet it should be remembered that the repose of an exterior depends very much on the expanses of plain walling, and that even a small change will have a telling effect. Nevertheless, the insertion of a well designed window in a large expanse of blank wall – for example in a gable-end – sometimes improves the appearance of the building.

In making a new window or door, proportion and architectural scale (which might be described as a subtle function of proportion and size) must be studied. It is nothing short of rank bad manners to introduce a foreign proportion into a façade. Windows built in stone are typically upright in shape, for the span of a stone lintel is limited, and the horizontal shape derived from the long spans made possible by steel or reinforced concrete does not usually combine well with them. In the exceptional case where a wall otherwise blank is not closely linked with other elevations, it is possible and sometimes preferable to treat the window in a modern manner. To enlarge a window by heightening or widening is risky, for proportion or scale or both may be affected: it is better to gain the extra glass area by forming a double or triple window designed on the pattern of the original.

Repairs or alterations to an old roof raise a general question of style. The Scottish climate, the plenty of some materials

D

and scarcity of others, together with less tangible factors, have produced a distinctive tradition in roofing (*fig.* 1). The form and finish of the roof have such a telling effect on the appear-

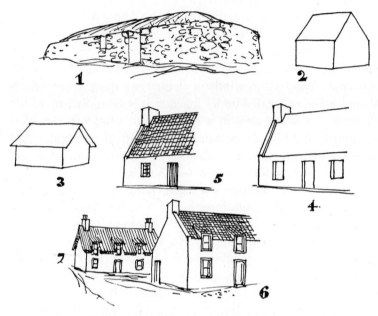

FIG. I.   Walls and Roof in the Scottish tradition.

The formal relationship of walls and roof in the stone-built Hebridean black house (1) and the gabled house (2) which developed on the mainland, contrasts sharply with the form (3) characteristic of timber-framed or mud-built houses and the tradition derived from them. It persists throughout the Scottish tradition (4) and is often made the more emphatic by colour and texture (5).

The sketch of (existing) identical houses shows the drastic change made when the native form (6) is replaced by a roof of alien type (7).

ance of a building that if this tradition is ignored the character of the reconstructed house will be drastically changed. In Scottish vernacular building, from the Hebridean black house to the cottage and burgh house of the 1800's, there has been a distinct tendency to marry walls and roof into a strong, almost sculptural, unity. Projections at eaves and gables are suppressed and the surface of the wall is continued into that of the roof with the least possible interruption. The conception is radically different from that of the roof as a hat resting on the walls: it is rather that of the hooded cloak, where cloak (walls) and hood (roof) are parts, if specialised ones, of one single protective covering. Features which belong to the hat construction, such as gable bargeboards, pronounced bell-cast, and overhanging eaves, are alien to this Scottish tradition which insists on simple planes and a clear emphasis on the single shape of the building as opposed to expression of its parts. The eaves are kept close and tight to the wall-head, and verges at gables are either treated in the same way or stopped against upstanding stone skews built on the gable wall-head. The piended roof is rare, except in minor roofs. (The half-piend half-apse of the Hebridean black house resulted from the difficulty of building a true gable in unhewn stones, and its effect is scarcely that of a piend.) The gable is preferred, possibly because it simplifies roof framing, but also because its form better expresses the partnership of roof and wall. The vigour which we admire in Scottish vernacular architecture is very much bound up in the closeness of this relationship. Yet in following tradition it is not sufficient merely to reject alien forms, for there is the opposite danger of banal imitation – as witness the Baronial revival, which seemed to reach its apogee of spiritless copyism in its treatment of roofs. Here almost more than anywhere else it is necessary to grasp the spirit as well as the details of traditional forms.

The traits we have noted in roof design are also seen in the handling of dormer windows, which can be broadly classified in two types (*fig.* 2). The first is the half dormer, a window at eaves level, with a stone surround which is essentially part of the wall below. The second, which might be called the full dormer, is framed out in timber from the roof slope only. Both types are handled with the sculptural directness which we have noted as characteristic of traditional roofs. The stonework of the half dormer, though sometimes highly ornamented, firmly asserts its unity with the main wall below, and is joined to the dormer roof with the same summary simplicity as we find at the eaves and gables of the main roof. The full dormer is treated equally firmly as a part or modulation of the main roof: its proportion is low, its junctions with the main slope are smoothly detailed, its general shape tends to be soft (many fine

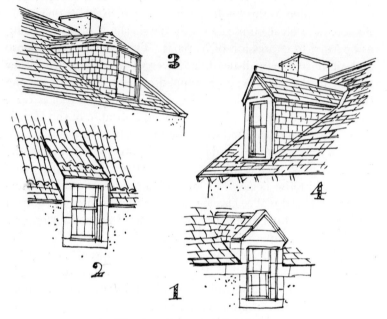

FIG. 2.   Dormer Windows.

1 and 2: Examples of half-dormers.
The full dormer (3) is one of several traditional types. Contrast the post-Georgian dormer (4) which abruptly intrudes on the roof.

examples are bow-fronted), and the window frame, closely surrounded by slates, is given the least possible emphasis. All this is in striking contrast to the typical Victorian dormer, with its high, narrow proportion (admitting a narrow arc of light into the room), its pretentious frame planted on the face of its roof: the whole thing an abrupt violation of the main slope.

Perhaps there is no clearer index to the decay of the tradition than this degeneration of dormer design, and in designing new dormers for an old roof you must be careful to go far enough back in your search for a good model.

3. Treatment of Damp

The greatest single threat to the soundness of a building is damp, and it therefore seems appropriate to begin our consideration of the practical details of reconstruction with this problem. The importance of keeping a building perfectly dry was not recognised until comparatively recent times, and although it is by no means the case that every old building is damp, it is fair to say that few if any are completely protected against it. No reconstruction job can be said to be properly done unless the utmost care has been taken to treat existing damp and to ensure that none will arise from some new source in the future.

Dampness and dilapidation of the more spectacular kinds are often caused by sheer neglect – by leaks in roofs, chimneyheads and copes, or cracks in lintels and sills, by broken or choked rones and drains, or by earth piled up high against external walls. Yet despite appearances all these things are relatively easy to put right in the course of ordinary repair work. What sets the more difficult problem is dampness which is caused by defects in design or construction. Rising damp, rain penetration through walls, and excessive condensation figure prominently under this heading and call for discussion in some detail.

Rising damp, as its name suggests, is caused by moisture from the damp ground under the building rising by capillary action in the fabric or by passing in vapour form across the spaces under suspended floors. In a modern building this is prevented by providing a continuous impermeable membrane called a damp-course (or, more properly, a damp-proof course) which isolates the superstructure from the ground and the underbuilding. The omission of a damp-course does not inevitably lead to rising damp – thousands of old buildings lack one yet are as dry as a bone – but a damp-course is an insurance against a very real risk. Even if the building to be reconstructed seems quite dry you must still assume the risk to be real, for reconstruction may itself upset a delicate balance of conditions which has hitherto prevented dampness.

In new work incidental to reconstruction, standard damp-proofing practice can and should be followed, but it is seldom possible to apply the same technique to the old work, and it is necessary to adopt special methods which give fully comparable results yet are at the same time practicable and economically feasible.

The first step is to make the wet ground – the source of the trouble – as dry as possible, by forming a land drain to trap the water before it passes under the building (*fig.* 3). As a further check to the seepage of water, a rendering of water-proof cement may be applied to the outer face of the main walls from their foundations up to a level six inches above ground level. The opportunities for such treatment vary from site to site, but in general everything which can be done to reduce the inflow of surface and subsoil water into the foundations is of value, though care must be taken not to dry out the ground *below* foundation level, for in most soils this would cause shrinkage and settlement.

The cost of inserting a damp-course in a thick stone wall is prohibitive, and other means of controlling rising damp must be adopted. Since capillary movement of water is not affected by gravity, the only check to the rise of damp is the evaporation which takes place at the wall faces. Evaporation at the inside face may be objectionable, but that at the outside face is harmless and should be encouraged – which means that the finish of the outside face from about six inches above ground level should always be permeable. If the wall is wet enough to justify the cost, the evaporation surface may be increased by

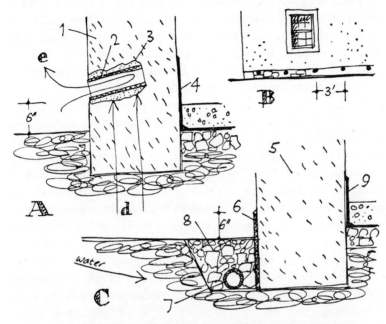

FIG. 3. The Checking of Rising Damp.

A, B: Section and elevation showing the Knapen system of damp control. Holes are made in the wall (1) above ground level, and in each is placed a length of unglazed pipe (2) bedded in lime mortar (3). Damp (d) rising from the ground passes through the permeable mortar and pipe, and is carried off by air (e) circulating through the open end of the pipe. The internal damp-proofing (4) must be carried above the level of the pipes.

C: Water running down the site into a wall may be checked by excavating a trench to foundation level, applying a waterproof cement rendering (6) to the wall (5) and forming a trap-drain with unglazed pipe (7) and infill (8) of clean stones and gravel. The internal damp-proofing (9) must be carried above the level of the outer skirt of waterproof mortar.

what are known as Knapen tubes. These are unglazed clay pipes inserted in a row near the base of the wall, each pipe being well bedded to the stone in lime mortar and laid so that one end is in the heart of the wall and the other open to the air at the outer wall-face. Moisture creeps from the stonework through the permeable mortar into the body of the pipe and is evaporated by the air circulating in the pipe. In recent years a new technique, based on the principle of electro-osmosis, has been developed. It makes use of electrodes buried in the wall and in the ground to generate a weak electric current which reverses the tendency of water to rise by capillarity.

Measures such as these effectively reduce the amount of dampness in the wall, but are not in themselves a complete substitute for a damp-course. It is necessary to take the further step of isolating the inside finish of the wall from the stonework. Whatever the state of the wall, its inner face must be sealed with a waterproofer up to a level at least six inches above ground, and if there is any rising damp already in the wall this sealing should be carried up to a level twelve inches above the highest apparent dampness. Where the wall-face is treated in this way, wood dooks must never be used: all fixings for skirtings and other finishings should be metal plugs. If possible these plugs should be fixed before the waterproofing is applied; if not, any holes left after piercing the waterproofing to insert the plugs must be carefully caulked and made good.

Internal partition walls may be tackled in various ways. Where only one side need be made dry, the partition may be rendered in waterproof cement on that side only, up to a level at least twelve inches above the highest sign of damp; but if both sides must be made dry it is worse than useless to seal them both in this way, for the moisture, unable to evaporate, will inevitably rise higher. If the partition is made of brick, it is not difficult to cut off the damp by inserting a horizontal damp-course (*fig.* 4). In a partition of four-and-a-half-inch thickness, this is done by removing the mortar from a horizontal joint near the base of the wall and substituting waterproofed cement mortar. By working in four stages, as shown in the sketch, this can be done without endangering the wall. A similar method can be applied to thicker partitions with one difference, that a whole course of bricks must be taken out (since it is not practicable to rake out a single joint to sufficient depth) and replaced with impervious engineering bricks bedded solidly in water-proof mortar. Recently a new technique has been developed to replace these methods, in which a hand- or

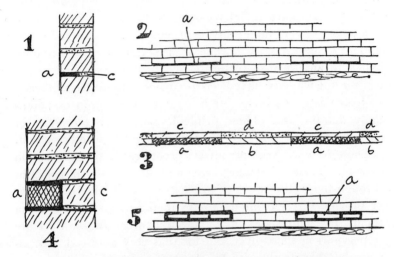

FIG. 4.   Inserting a Damp-course in Brick Walls.
The section of a half-brick wall (1) shows the first stage of the process, in which part of a bed-joint (a) is raked out and packed with waterproof mortar, in alternate stretches along the wall (2). The plan (3) shows how the process is repeated in sequence (a, b, c, d) until the whole bed-joint has been replaced.
    A thicker wall (4 and 5) is dealt with in the same manner except that a whole course of bricks is replaced.

power-operated saw is used to cut right through a horizontal joint, and a metal or felt damp-course in two-foot lengths is pushed into the slot as the sawing proceeds. The average rate of progress is about six feet per hour in four-and-a-half-inch brick-work and four feet in nine-inch brickwork, and the cost is about half that of the older methods.
    In rubble stone partitions there are no continuous horizontal

joints and the insertion of a damp-course is difficult if not impossible. The best way out is to strap and plaster the wall in the manner described later in this section, using metal plugs in preference to wood dooks wherever positive signs of damp are found, and ventilating the cavity behind the plasterwork.

The damp-proofing of floors must of course be properly integrated with that of walls and partitions, for any gap in the defences will sooner or later jeopardise the success of the work as a whole. Every floor must be provided with a perfectly continuous damp-proof membrane or *solum* damp-course carefully joined to any vertical sealing which has been applied to the walls in the ways we have been discussing. Again, no timbers – such as joists – must be left in contact with damp or potentially damp walls. These principles, and the techniques of carrying them out, are considered in detail in a later section.

Plain stone walls are not always proof against the penetration of rain. Through-bonders (i.e. long stones which go right through the wall from front to back) act as channels for water or provide direct capillary routes in the mortar surrounding them. The whinstones often found in Scottish rubble work are impervious in themselves, but for that very reason do not always bond perfectly with the mortar, and leave slightly open joints which conduct water with astonishing rapidity. For these and other reasons the solid stone wall cannot be trusted to keep out water, and its efficiency as a protector depends finally upon its finishes.

The immediately obvious plan is to treat the outside face of the wall with cement, paint, or some other waterproof material. Though it is useful in certain circumstances, the method is open to several objections (*fig.* 5). Rain-water runs swiftly down the impervious face, causing extra wear and tear, and streaking and staining at projections. The success of the waterproofing depends entirely on the permanence of the material and the perfection of the workmanship. The slightest defect will draw water into the backing by capillary action, and this water,

trapped behind the waterproofing, will either travel to the
inside face to wreak damage there or will remain near the
outer face. If it remains it will probably freeze in cold weather,
and in freezing will expand and throw off the waterproof
coating.

Most of these objections disappear if the waterproofing is
applied to the inner face of the wall. The success of the treatment still depends very much on material and workmanship,

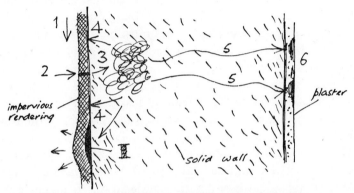

FIG. 5.   The Weakness of a Waterproof Harling.

Rainwater (1) running down the face is drawn by capillary force
into any fine crack or defect (2) and soaks into the backing (3).
Escape by outward evaporation (4) is prevented by the impervious
harling, and moisture gradually seeps through the wall (5) to
appear as damp patches (6) in the internal plaster.
     In winter, moisture trapped under the harling may freeze, and
its expansion into ice (I) tends to burst the harling away from the
stone.

but the waterproofing has a better chance of escaping damage.
Yet since the body of the wall remains damp, it will the more
rapidly conduct heat away from the inside face, and condensation on this cool surface is likely to be excessive. Another
objection is that it is difficult to get fixing for internal finishings
– such as skirtings – without breaking the essential continuity
of the waterproofing. To mitigate condensation, the waterproof undercoat should be finished with a skimming coat of

absorptive material such as vermiculite plaster or lime putty mixed with coarse sand. The fixing difficulty can be got over by using metal plugs placed in position before waterproofing the wall.

Paradoxically enough, the best treatment involves the use of no waterproofing at all (*fig. 6*). An absorptive rendering of lime or lime-cement mortar applied to the outer face of the wall will soak up water like a sponge but easily discharge it again by evaporation into the air. Protected by this first line of defence, the wall will remain relatively dry; but to make certain that seepage is stopped, the plasterwork must be separated from the masonry by an air-space. The traditional way of forming this air-space is to mount the plasterwork on wooden straps fixed to dooks driven into the wall. The dooks must be of metal or of rot-resistant wood and be cut off at least a quarter of an inch from the wall-face so that the straps are kept clear of the stone at every point, and the straps themselves should be treated with a non-staining preservative, preferably by a pressurised process. Nowadays plaster lath (plasterboard made in narrow strips) is the usual base for the plasterwork. If metal lath is used it must be of a type protected against corrosion, and hessian should be stretched over the strapping before the lath is fixed to prevent the plaster squeezing through the lath so far as to bridge the air-space behind. This method of strapping walls is recommended as satisfactory in all conditions by the current *British Standard Code of Practice for Rubble Walls*; it is easily carried out and provides good thermal insulation. For the extra cost of about a shilling a yard an even higher standard of thermal insulation can be obtained by using a plaster lath backed with aluminium foil.

Another way of making the isolated inner skin is to build a thin wall of light-weight blocks two inches clear of the stone-work, finished with plaster in the normal manner. This wall must be properly damp-coursed, and the cavity between the inner and outer walls must be kept clear of mortar droppings.

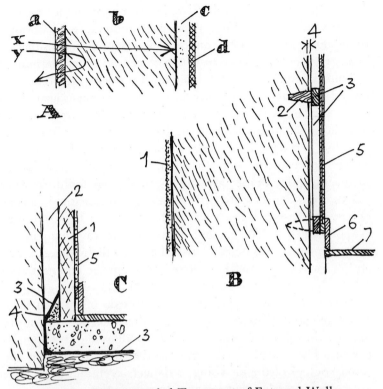

Fig. 6.　Recommended Treatment of External Walls.

A: The construction is in four parts: (*a*) a permeable outer rendering, (*b*) the solid wall, (*c*) an air-space and (*d*) an inner lining.
Direct penetration (*x*) is stopped by the air-space, while the permeable rendering allows water to evaporate harmlessly (*y*) from
the wall.

B: The construction in detail: the cement-lime harling (1) is
given a rough surface to check the run of water down the face;
the rot-proofed dooks (2) support 2″ × 1″ wood strapping so that
it is at all points at least a quarter-of-an-inch clear of the stonework; the finishings of the inner lining consist of plaster on plaster
lath (5) and wood skirting (6) above the floor (7).

C: An alternative form of inner lining consists of a wall of 2″
clinker concrete blocks (1) separated from the stone wall by a 2″
cavity (2) and finished with plaster (5). The damp-course (3)
must be carried up the edge of the floor slab and over a cement
fillet (4) to protect the base of the lining. All things considered,
this treatment is not superior to the traditional one shown in B.

The method is certainly effective, but compared with strapped plasterwork it is wasteful of floor-space and clumsy in working round doors and windows; and since it is not markedly superior in any respect there seems little to commend it as an alternative.

Timber requires so little dampness in order to rot that prolonged exposure to moist air is practically as dangerous to it as direct contact with damp earth or stone. Since wood is permeable, air can percolate into it, and if the air is moist enough and the exposure long enough the wood will become wet enough to favour the growth of rot. This danger easily arises in spaces under timber ground floors. In old buildings such spaces are often unventilated and the ground below innocent of any damp-proof covering, with the result that moisture evaporating from the ground can gather in the stagnant air and permeate the timbers above. The air will, in effect, act as a pipe conveying water in vapour form from the ground to the wood. Now it may often be true that this has been going on for a century or more without any outbreaks of rot, but since a fresh infection of spores or any slight alteration in temperature may set up rot at any time, it is folly to allow the condition to persist. The remedy is to ventilate the space to prevent the water content of the air rising to danger level, and to seal the ground with a *solum* damp-course to reduce the evaporation of moisture into the air.

Moist air is also the cause of condensation troubles in buildings (*fig.* 7). At any given temperature, air cannot contain more than a certain definite amount of water vapour. When the actual moisture content equals this amount the air is said to be saturated. This saturation point varies directly with the temperature: cool air cannot carry as much vapour as warm air, and if warm air is cooled down it will sooner or later reach a temperature at which it is saturated and condensation will begin. This critical temperature is called the 'dew-point' for air of that particular humidity. The familiar misting of windows on a cold day is an example of this process: the warm air

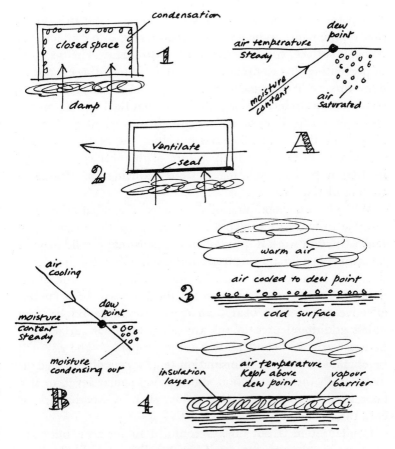

FIG. 7. Condensation Causes and Cures.

A: Condensation caused by rising humidity:
    1 – Damp entering a closed space raises the humidity to saturation level and moisture condenses out on the enclosing surfaces. The cure (2) is to bring in fresh air to prevent this build-up of moisture, and to seal off the damp as effectively as possible.

B: Condensation caused by cooling of air:
    3 – Dew forms when warm air meets a cold surface. One remedy (4) is to insulate the surface (e.g.: by an 'anticondensation paint') so that the air is no longer cooled by it. A vapour barrier is necessary to prevent water vapour percolating through the insulation and condensing below it.

of the room, coming close to the cold glass, is cooled past its dew-point and some of the vapour it is carrying comes out as dew on the pane. Whenever warm air comes into contact with a cooler surface, condensation is likely to occur. The best way of preventing it is to prevent the contact, but if this cannot be done three other remedies may be applied either singly or in combination: to increase ventilation so that the humidity of the room air is kept low; or to increase air movement so that the air passing the cold surface has not time to cool to dewpoint; or, thirdly, to raise the temperature of the surface, either by heating it or by insulating it, thus reducing the degree of cooling of the air.

With this understanding of the nature of condensation, it is possible to foresee and avoid its occurrence. For example, in reconstruction work it quite often happens that a solid ground floor must be laid at or near ground level. On a dry site such a floor will have a high heat insulation value, but if the site is damp the wet ground underneath the floor will be a far less effective reservoir of heat than drier ground would be, and unless additional precautions are taken the floor surface will be less warm and condensation more probable. The risk will be obviated if a layer of insulation (e.g. vermiculite screed) is included in the construction above damp-course level, or if a floor finish of high insulation value, such as wood block or cork tile, is chosen.

Condensation is not always confined to surfaces, but may occur within the structure itself (*fig.* 8). For example, the floor treatment we have just mentioned will certainly prevent surface condensation, but it will do little to prevent water vapour from percolating through the floor insulation to come into contact with the colder material below, where it would condense above the damp-course and possibly cause trouble. It is always necessary to provide a vapour barrier (a plastic floor-seal or the waterproof adhesive used to fix the floor finish) on the *warm* side of the insulation so that the air meets an impervious surface

PLATE 7.   PROVOST ROSS'S HOUSE, ABERDEEN

Restored by the National Trust for Scotland, with aid from
the Local Authority, the Historic Buildings Council for
Scotland, Associated British Cinemas Ltd., and the Pilgrim
Trust. The very magnificence of this restoration makes
more bitter the reflection that many fine internal finishings,
which had survived for centuries, were lost by sheer neglect
in the last few years before the National Trust stepped in.

PLATE 8. THE MANSE, CANONGATE, EDINBURGH

Restored by the Canongate Kirk, this house stands in a
historic street which is being extensively restored by the
Local Authority and other bodies.

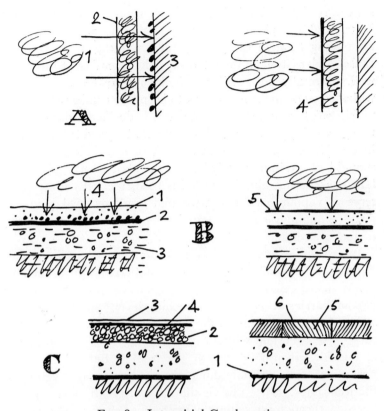

FIG. 8.   Interstitial Condensation.

A: Warm moist air (1) percolating through a permeable lining (2) may cause condensation on the cold inner face of the external wall (3). It may be prevented by applying an impervious seal or 'vapour barrier' (4) at the inside face.

B: The same trouble can occur in a floor, particularly if the sub-floor (3) is damp: warm vapour (4) passing through the material or the joints of the floor covering (1) may condense on the relatively cold surface of the damp-course (2). The remedy is again a vapour barrier (5) at the surface, though if the covering is a poor insulator, some additional insulation may be necessary to effect a complete cure.

C: Two typical floor constructions show how interstitial condensation may be prevented by a barrier on the *warm* side of the insulating layer: (1) damp-course, (2) insulating screed (e.g. vermiculite concrete), (3) floor finish with a mastic bedding (4) acting as vapour barrier; (5) shows a wood-block floor with an oil-seal (6) as vapour barrier.

kept warm by the insulation behind or below it. Where a wall is strapped and plastered, there is always the risk that warm air passing through the plaster and across the air-space may cause condensation on the relatively cold inner face of the stone wall. Normally, the small gaps incidental to the construction will allow enough air movement to keep this condensation well within safe limits; but where the wall is decidedly damp (and therefore cold) positive ventilation should be provided by grilles in the skirting, and a vapour barrier, such as building paper, should be fixed immediately behind the plasterwork. If plaster lath backed with aluminium foil is used, the foil will at once serve as vapour barrier and thermal insulator. Oil paint, if properly maintained, is also an efficient vapour barrier. Distemper is useless.

Interstitial condensation of this kind can also do serious damage to flat roofs covered with an impervious finish such as metal or roofing-felt. Again it should be prevented by a vapour barrier at or just above ceiling level. Similar condensation sometimes occurs on the underside of slates or tiles when these have been laid without underslating felt. The provision of this felt will usually obviate the trouble, but if the roof is not being altered the only thing that can be done is to ventilate the roof-space. Since this ventilation will greatly increase the heat-loss through the ceilings of the rooms below, good thermal insulation at ceiling level should be supplied to compensate.

It sometimes happens that dampness is attributed to condensation or to rising damp when in fact it is caused by the presence in the wall of certain salts which have the property of extracting moisture from the air – sea-salt introduced in sand taken from a beach is one common example. Dampness caused by condensation appears all over a surface, rising damp shows in a distinct area often edged along the top with a band of efflorescence, but dampness caused by these hygroscopic salts tends to be patchy and to vary with the weather, becoming worse just before rain. The only way of treating the salts is to encourage them to leach out of the wall. Patches of half-crystallised salt should be wiped off the wall, and the leaching can be accelerated by putting on poultices of wet whiting and removing them when dry. If these measures are not wholly effective, recourse to strapped plasterwork may be necessary. Any such strapping must be kept quite clear of the wall-face and the wood must be treated with preservative by a pressurised process.

4. Treatment of Dry Rot

Dry rot, despite its name, is caused by damp, and is therefore connected with the general problem of dampness which we have been discussing. We do not propose to embark on a detailed description of its nature and treatment (which are too complex a subject for a book of this kind) but merely to draw attention to a few salient points which are of particular importance in the present connection – the general character of the rot, its detection, and the broad principles of defence against it. For a fuller discussion the reader is referred to the Bulletin *Dry Rot in Wood*, published by the Department of Scientific and Industrial Research.

The rotting of wood is caused by fungi. Many of these fungi only attack wet or damp wood, setting up 'wet rot' which can be stopped quite simply by eliminating the dampness and cutting away the infected timber. The distinguishing mark of the fungi which set up 'dry rot' is that once they have started to grow in damp timber they are able to spread further and to attack dry timber. Hence their virulence, the difficulty in tracing them, and the need to be exceedingly thorough in dealing with them.

Dampness alone will not cause dry rot: the infection must be there, the temperature must be right, and the fungus needs air to breathe. It follows that if a building is damp you ought not to rush to the conclusion that dry rot will be present: it is sufficient to assume that the risk is there, to keep a sharp look-out for any symptoms and to take care, in all the alteration work you do, that you do not create or perpetuate conditions which could encourage an attack. For it also follows that, even supposing there are no signs of active attack, the fungus may be present in a dormant state, ready to develop if opportunity offers. Knowledge of dry rot is of direct importance in dealing with an outbreak of it, but it is equally, if indirectly, important as an influence on general design, which can never be called sound unless it takes the threat of rot seriously.

The Dry Rot Fungus (*Merulius lachrymans*) thrives on very little moisture and spreads with immense vigour. Grey strands run over surfaces and through plaster and masonry, seeking timber to feed on. In places they may develop into thick sheets of silver-grey skin blotched with sharp yellow or lilac, and when the fungus is mature it produces fleshy fruit-bodies which discharge millions of reddish-brown spores, spreading the infection through the building and perhaps for miles around. The White Pore Fungus (*Poria vaillanti*) is distinguished by its white strands, white or cream-coloured sheets and white plate-like fruit-bodies. It likes the same conditions as *Merulius* but is much less active in spreading and is to that extent the easier to eradicate. Several other fungi occur less frequently in buildings; like *Poria* they are much less virulent than *Merulius*. You should therefore take care to identify the fungus correctly before estimating the extent of the treatment you may have to apply.

Sometimes the strands or the fruit-body show on the surface, but more often the growth is hidden and is betrayed only by its smell or by signs in the surface woodwork, such as warping, cracking, softness, or the dead sound produced when it is struck. At the least suspicion, the woodwork should be taken down, and if more evidence is found behind it the search must be continued until the full extent of the growth is discovered and its probable cause or causes established. This is not easy to do – especially if you are dealing with *Merulius*, whose strands can penetrate walls and run for long distances under concrete and asphalt, and do not immediately die when cut off, but lie for a while ready to seize any opportunity to start a fresh outbreak. You must take no risks, but pursue the search regardless of incidental damage to structure or finishings.

Once you have ascertained the full extent of the attack, every scrap of infected or suspect timber must be removed, and the infection sterilised by burning-off all adjacent stone or brickwork with a blowlamp and treating all surfaces with sodium fluoride or other fungicide. Then the dampness which started the outbreak must be eliminated. This might sound as if it were the end of the matter, but since in the nature of things you can never be certain that sterilisation is complete, you must go further and adopt a scorched-earth policy, denying any lurking infection the food it needs, by substituting other materials for wood wherever possible and by making sure that any wood you have to use in the vicinity is treated with preservative, is dry when fixed, and is kept dry (by damp-course and ventilation) thereafter. It is also advisable to leave inspection panels (for example, removable floorboards) so that you may inspect the hidden work periodically until you are satisfied, perhaps a year later, that the infection has been killed. The treatment of dry rot is in fact a chain of processes – removal, sterilisation, and defensive design – each of which demands close attention and scrupulous workmanship.

5. External Walls

Though the popular idea of the strength and durability of 'solid stone walls' is often exaggerated, it is true that most of the stonework of the period we are considering was built with a margin of safety sufficient to enable it to withstand much mutilation and neglect, and to survive in spite of occasional intrinsic weakness caused by ignorant design or scamped workmanship. Unless it has been very badly damaged by decay or settlement, its repair will be an economic proposition in the sense that it will be cheaper – and usually much cheaper – than demolition and replacement.

In assessing the strength of an old stone wall, particularly if it is of rubble work, the state of its mortar is a prime consideration. You will find that the mortar is either lime mortar or – in primitive buildings – something little better than mud. Sometimes trial holes will show that it is soft and crumbling, looking far from impressive to eyes accustomed to the strong mortars in use today. Yet you must not jump to conclusions too quickly, for the real question is not whether the wall is as strong as it could be but whether it is as strong as it needs to be. In small domestic buildings the external walls are seldom loaded to capacity, and the stresses may be as little as a quarter of the safe maximum. Since stone walls are about twice as thick as their brick counterparts, the comparable stresses due to the weights of roof and floors are halved. Furthermore, since the stone wall is thicker and therefore stiffer than the brick wall, the mortar in it can carry a higher stress – or, putting the same thing another way, the mortar in a thick wall need not be intrinsically as strong as that in a slender wall under the same conditions of load. For all these reasons, superficial comparison with brickwork mortar is highly misleading, and you should rather judge the case strictly in terms of the actual loads and stresses. Generally speaking, the state of the wall as a whole is a fair guide: if it has stood for a century or more without serious failure it is likely to continue to do so, provided you give it proper protection and maintenance and do not materially increase its loading by your alterations to the house. In doubtful cases, a wall can be made secure by injecting liquid mortar into it. The principal points of this technique of grouting are shown in the sketch (*fig.* 9).

Cracks in a wall indicate either settlement of foundation or

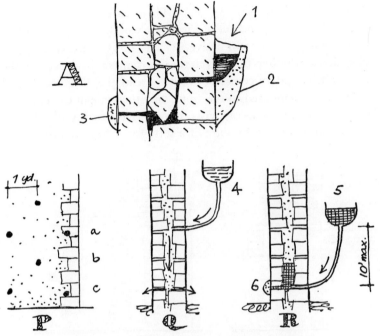

FIG. 9.   Grouting the Hearting of a Wall.

A: Hand-grouting is used to fill isolated cavities. Holes are made
  through joints of face-work above and below the cavity, and a
  funnel or 'swallow's nest' of clay (2) is formed at the upper one.
  The cavity is first washed out by pouring water into the swallow's
  nest, then the lower hole is plugged with clay (3) and the cavity
  filled by running-in a grout (1) composed of equal parts of
  cement and fine sand mixed with water.

When the hearting is generally unsound, pressure-grouting is
resorted to:

P: Access holes at about 3-foot centres in staggered rows are formed
  in both sides of the wall.

Q: A section of hearting is washed out by running water from a
  grouting-pan (4) by flexible hose into a hole at level (a). This
  must be done with care and judgement: excessive washing may
  cause hearting to collapse.

R: Grout (5) is then run in at level (c). Pressure must not be high, or
  the wall may burst. Leaks are plugged with clay (6). When grout
  rises to level (b) the work is stopped until the cement sets, when
  grouting is resumed at hole (b).

Grouting is done over short lengths of wall, working in a sequence
similar to that used in underpinning (see Fig. 13).

excessive local stresses (*fig.* 10). Their seriousness, from your point of view, depends very much on whether they are old or recent, long dead or still active. Where there is any doubt, you can check whether there is active movement by bridging the crack with a dab of cement or (better) a strip of thin roughened glass firmly cemented to the stone on either side of the crack: if such a tell-tale cracks or twists, movement is taking place. But often you can infer the date of a settlement from details of the

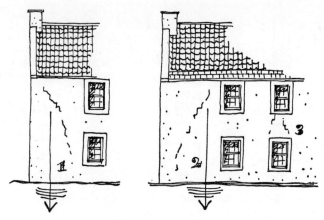

FIG. 10.   Diagnosis of Settlement Cracks.

The slope of crack (1) indicates that a settlement has occurred to the left of it; the cause of crack (2) lies below its highest point. Cracking at (3) is typical of failure of a lintel beneath it.

adjoining work: if, for example, a wooden window frame has been shaped to fit a canted lintel, the inference is that the settlement happened before the window was fitted and has not recurred since. In normal circumstances, settlement does not continue indefinitely, for in itself it tends to relieve the conditions which have caused it and, once stopped, does not start again unless and until some change takes place in the supporting subsoil or the adjacent walls.

Inactive cracks need not arouse great concern. They threaten the weathertightness of the wall more than its stability. Small

cracks may be sealed with mortar well worked in, but larger
ones should be built up, not merely on face but to their full
depth. In a harled wall this infilling need only be block-
bonded at intervals to the stonework, but when the wall is to be

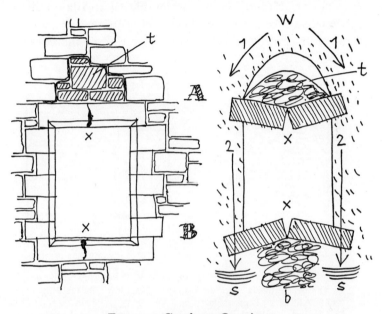

FIG. 11. Cracks at Openings.

A: When a lintel cracks (x) the stonework above it tends to act as
an arch diverting the load (w) downwards and sideways ($1, 1$) to
either side of the opening, leaving only a small mass (t) to be
supported by the lintel itself.

B: The loads ($2, 2$) at the sides of an opening may cause settlements
(s, s) under the ends of the sill, but leave the unloaded walling (b)
below the opening unaffected: the sill, being supported by (b)
at the centre but forced downwards by ($2, 2$) at the ends, will
bend and ultimately crack at (x).

pointed you will have to take down more of the adjoining face-
work so that the new stones may be properly bonded in to
match the rest.

A cracked sill is caused by the wall at one or both sides of the
opening settling more than the lightly loaded panel of walling

under the sill: the built-in ends of the sill are pressed downwards so that its middle part is arched upwards and cracks (*fig.*
11). The crack is of no structural importance, but it must be
sealed up. The structural effect of a cracked lintel varies with
circumstances. If there is any considerable area of plain walling
immediately above the lintel, this panel of stonework acts as a
natural arch carrying the load to either side of the opening

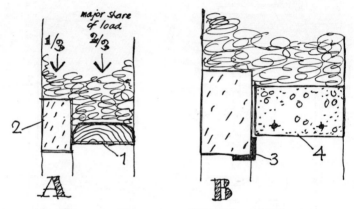

FIG. 12.   Treatment of Defective Lintels.
A: The back-lintel (1) carries most of the load: if it fails, cracking
of face-lintel (2) is probable.
B: Cracked face-lintel is supported by a concealed metal angle
bearer (3), while the back-lintel is replaced by reinforced concrete (4).

below, leaving the lintel itself to carry few if any of the stones
above it, and the crack has therefore no material effect on the
general stability of the wall. The case is different if floor joists or
roof timbers are bearing on the wall only a short distance above
the opening, for then the failure of the lintel leaves the floor or
roof with that much less support. Openings usually have a face
lintel on the outside and a back lintel behind it (*fig.* 12). The
latter may be as thick as two-thirds of the wall thickness, and is
in fact the main load-carrier. Nine times out of ten the failure of
a face lintel is due to the previous failure of its back lintel. Some

old builders had a bad habit of making the back lintel in timber, which by shrinking or decaying burdens the other with an excessive share of the load. The defective back lintel – indeed any timber lintel, decayed or not – should be cut out and replaced by reinforced concrete. The cracked face lintel

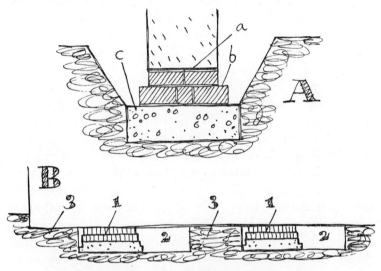

FIG. 13.   Underpinning a Wall.

A: Cross-section showing new concrete foundation (*c*) and brick footings (*b*) inserted under old wall-base (*a*).

B: Longitudinal section of wall showing method of working: Short lengths (1) are completed and allowed to set before ground is excavated for the second stage (2), and the remainder of the ground (3) is left undisturbed until (2) is completed. The end of a section is left toothed so that the next may be bonded to it.

may be replaced by a new stone or made good by jacking it up level and securing it with a metal angle bearer as shown in the sketch.

If active cracks indicate that the building as a whole is subsiding, the necessary treatment would be so difficult and expensive that it could not be justified save in the case of a historic monument, but if the cracks show that settlement is local, the cost of securing the walls may be within reasonable limits. The cause of the settlement is that the pressure per square foot of the foundation is too much for the underlying soil, and the principle of the treatment is to increase the area of the foundation until the pressure is reduced to one which the soil can support. The method is to work on successive short lengths of the wall, excavating under the old foundation, forming a new concrete foundation of adequate width, and underpinning the wall by building off the new foundation up to the underside of the old one (*fig.* 13).

When you find that a wall is out of plumb, you need not immediately conclude that it is unsafe. A well-tried working rule is that so long as the vertical line through its centre of gravity passes within the middle third of its base, a wall may be considered to be stable (*fig.* 14). Thus a wall eighteen inches thick is unlikely to topple over so long as its head is not more than five inches out of plumb with its base. If its actual tilt is less than half the maximum safe tilt and if there is nothing to suggest that the tilt is actively increasing, a wall may be safely left as it is; but in all other cases leaning walls ought to be made secure. At first sight, buttressing might seem a suitable means of support, but far from securing the wall it would in fact make matters worse, for the cause of tilting is undue pressure on a weak subsoil, and a buttress would add more weight without materially reducing the pressure. The correct treatment is to underpin the wall with a wider foundation.

Before leaving the subject, we would repeat the point made earlier, that new settlement can be caused by injudicious site drainage. In many old houses, the foundation of the wall is simply a course of big stones laid without much ceremony on the topsoil itself; and if open-jointed tile drains are run close to the wall and below foundation level, they may cause the ground immediately under the foundation to dry out and shrink, with obvious results.

Surface decay of stone may be caused by frost action on incorrectly bedded stones. Sedimentary stones are laminated in structure, and when the stone is built into the wall it should be

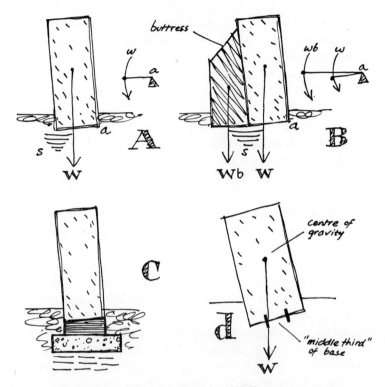

FIG. 14. Leaning Walls.

Section A shows a wall tilting because of weak ground (s) at one side of the base. The thrust (W) of the wall tends to bear more heavily upon (s) and to act as an overturning force relative to the firmer foundation at (a). The addition of a buttress (at B) merely adds its weight (Wb) to the load on (s) and increases the tendency to overturning. But by underpinning the wall with a new wide foundation (at C), the load may be spread and the pressure on (s) reduced to safe stress.

d: The Middle-third Rule: so long as the tilt does not exceed the limit shown, the wall will not overturn.

laid on its natural bed with these laminations horizontal – in other words, the stone should lie in the wall as it lay in the rock.

Sometimes – either because the natural bed was not clearly marked or because the builder was lazy – a stone is found to be face-bedded, that is, laid with the laminations upright and parallel to the wall-face. Each winter the rain-water which has seeped into the face of the stone freezes and splits off the outermost lamination, and as years pass the process repeats itself lamination by lamination until there is no sound stone left. The best thing to do with it is to cut it out and put in a new stone. The cheaper but less sightly alternative is to patch it with a mortar made of crushed stone, but this is useless unless it is done with care. All unsound stone must be cut away, and the mortar given a good key by hacking the surface of the stone and by fixing copper reinforcing wires to nails driven into the wall.

The other principal type of surface decay is caused by atmospheric pollution or by the leaching out of salts present in the stone or in the bedding mortar. Salts are deposited on or just beneath the surface of the stone, and form a hard skin which blisters and flakes off, leaving a fresh surface exposed to further attack. Salts of this kind are present in cement, and for this reason lime mortar rather than cement mortar should be used in building or repairing stonework. The decay can be checked by washing the stone from time to time with clean water (soap or detergent must *not* be used), or by painting it with oil paint after it has been cleaned. There are many proprietary stone-preservative solutions on the market which give fair results, though even colourless solutions change the colour of the stone slightly. The type used must be chosen with care, for not all preservatives suit every type of stone, and the stone must be cleaned before the solution is applied. The treatment is not permanent, and will have to be renewed from time to time.

The use of stone for the rebuilding, repair, or extension of stone buildings is obviously desirable, but it is complicated by conditions in the building industry. The problems are particularly acute in the case of the small job which does not justify special contract arrangements or attract the notice of specialist contractors. There is a shortage of skilled tradesmen, and many contractors cannot readily command such labour. Again, some contractors, unfamiliar with stone buildings, make tenders which are more in the nature of wild guesses than fair offers, and others frankly admit that they price high to cover what they think is a very uncertain cost. The would-be user of stone is often put under strong pressure to abandon his intention, yet he ought not to allow himself to be put off by such parrot-cries as: 'There aren't any stonemasons left in Scotland,' and: 'Build in stone? It'll cost you the earth!' There are still competent tradesmen in every part of the country, even a few young ones, and although new stonework is more expensive than comparable walling in brick, the cost should not be astronomical. A fair price for eighteen-inch rubble stonework should lie somewhere between two and three times that of eleven-inch cavity brickwork, and if a reasonable tender cannot be obtained from a local contractor, the recruitment of direct labour may prove economic and worth the additional trouble of being your own contractor.

Second-hand stone from ruinous buildings in the neighbourhood has much to commend it and in some respects is to be preferred to new stone. Not only will it cost less, but if – as is likely – it came from the same quarry as the building you are reconstructing, it will show the same colours, textures, and characteristic shapes, and will build and weather in much the same way. It has the drawback that it lacks the 'quarry sap' which makes new stone easy to dress and plays an important part in its weathering. For this reason, re-working of second-hand stone should be avoided. Fortunately there was in the past a rough and ready standardisation of lintels, sills, and rybats, and you will be unlucky if you cannot find and salvage dressed stones which will fit into their new positions with little or no re-working.

Careless or unsuitable pointing will ruin the appearance of stonework and affect its durability. No pointing will last unless there is a good body of mortar in it, and the first essential is to prepare the joints by raking out to a depth of at least an inch, or preferably two inches. The colour of the pointing should suit the stone, and its texture should not be smooth and shiny but lively and varied. You will find that good appearance will follow naturally from the use of those materials and techniques which are best calculated to ensure durability. The sand should be chosen for colour and must be sharp and well graded up to very coarse – if it contains irregular particles, such as small pebbles or broken shells, so much the better. A fine clayey mason's sand is worse than useless: the kind needed is often marketed as concretor's sand, though some of these may have to be mixed with a proportion of a bright rendering sand to improve colour and workability. The mortar should be about the same strength as the bedding mortar, and be based on lime – either a straight lime mortar (e.g. 2:3 lime-sand) or a gauged one (e.g. 1:2:8 cement-lime-sand). It is bad practice to use a strong cement mortar, for besides containing injurious salts it is ugly, and also tends to form capillary cracks which draw water into the joint – it has happened more than once that when such mortar was raked out water flowed visibly from behind it. The recessed or 'hungry' style of pointing has been fashionable in restoration work, but it is affected in appearance and technically bad because it leaves little ledges to hold water. Raised 'strap' pointing is even more objectionable on the same grounds. From all points of view it is best to finish the pointing flush with the edge of the stone (particularly the top edge) but it must be kept off the face so that the shape of each stone is clearly shown. If the edges of the stone are rounded or irregular, a slight recessing (perhaps one-eighth inch) will be necessary. Finally, the finish is important: the lazy man's 'leather' (usually a scrap of old inner tube) leaves a most unpleasant smeared surface, whereas the proper method of brushing with a

PLATE 9

24 COLLEGE STREET
St ANDREWS

Restored by the University of St Andrews. This building (and others shown in the Plates) would look even better if it were harled in the traditional manner. The strong texture of the rubble stonework is competing with the pattern of the tiles and the dressed work at openings and gables, denying them their full decorative value.

PLATE 10.   PLEWLANDS, SOUTH QUEENSFERRY

Restored as housing by the National Trust for Scotland, with the aid of a public subscription, the Pilgrim Trust, and the Distillers Company Ltd. The house is the most prominent feature of the west end of the main street. Its restoration was hotly debated at the time, but when it was completed those who had opposed it admitted that it was justified by the result.

dry medium-soft bristle brush exposes the sand and gives a crisp surface which goes well with the stone and is resistant to cracking.

Looking ahead for a moment to the day when the garden is planted, do not attempt to grow ivy on a wall. Its powerful adventitious roots grow into the joints, breaking out the mortar and letting in the water. If you must have a creeper, choose another, such as Virginia creeper, *Ampelopsis veitchii*, which uses suckers, not roots, to attach itself to the wall.

Today, when stonework as a symbol of the past has acquired a certain romantic glamour, we are only too ready to leave it uncovered, but traditional builders recognised that many – though by no means all – Scottish building stones need to be protected against the weather by some form of rendering or harling. So many old buildings have lost their original finish that it is unwise to assume too readily that an existing finish is either original or adequate. Raised margins round the openings or at the quoins (corner-stones) are fair indication that the building was intended to be harled. Even when such indications are absent the very style of the facework should make it obvious whether the original builder meant it to be admired or concealed. But whatever his intention, if there are any signs that the stone is not weather-resistant, your decision should be to harl it.

The old Scots harling differed from modern renderings both in composition and in application. Modern sands and gravels are sieved and washed at the quarry to ensure some consistency in composition and grading, but in the old days these materials were used just as they came from the pit or river-bed, and were very irregular in size and mixed in type. The binding agent was lime, not cement, and instead of being floated on to the wall with a large rectangular trowel, the harling was either thrown on or applied with a small pointed trowel. Differences in technique result in differences in appearance, and there is no doubt that the older type of finish suits stone buildings better

F

than any other. The irregular material lends liveliness to the surface, and the technique of dashing produces a finish which clings to the backing and preserves a vivid feeling of the stoniness of the wall beneath. The wisdom of using lime in preference to cement, and the virtues of a dashed rendering, are confirmed by modern building research, and there is therefore technical justification to add to aesthetic preference in deciding to use a modern version of the old finish.

Precise reproduction is probably impossible without going back to primitive materials, but if you choose the aggregates carefully, and win the co-operation of contractor and tradesman, you can get a very close approximation. The mortar should be composed of sharp sand graded up to very coarse and mixed with perhaps ten per cent of pebbles or gravel up to a quarter or three-eighth inch in size, lime soaked in water for at least sixteen hours before use, and a small quantity of cement to speed up the initial set (typical proportions might be one part cement, two parts lime, eight parts mixed aggregate, all measured by volume when dry). When used for dashing the mix must be just wet enough to spread when thrown on to the wall, but not so wet as to prevent the material from standing up and showing a firm crisp texture. Deliberate patterning is quite out of place: if the consistency is right, an interesting and lively surface will be produced quite naturally by the technique itself.

The dressed stone margins provided as 'stops' for the harling may be raised above the rest of the stonework, or flush with it. Relieved margins are seldom raised high enough to accommodate the three-quarter-inch thickness of a modern floated rendering, which would need to be thinned or feathered-off where it meets them. But it is one of the characteristics of the technique of dashing that the material adheres to the backing much more strongly than it does when floated, and you may take advantage of this to keep down the general thickness of the harling to suit the relief of the margins. When the margins are not raised, feathering-off is however inevitable, and is certainly to be preferred to cutting off the full thickness of the harling in an abrupt line at the edge of the dressed stone. Where the harling is thinned in this way, it is particularly important to secure a good key for it; and it is worth going to the extra expense of clouring back the stone face immediately beside the margin to reduce the degree of feathering-off required.

The traditional finish to lime harling and, often enough, to pointed rubblework was lime wash. Untinted, it produces a white of peculiar brilliance (a perfect foil to slates and dressed stonework) but there are also local traditions in the use of colour which ought to be better known than they are – the snuff colour of Musselburgh and the pink of Dunblane for example, or the daring polychromaticism found in east-coast fishing villages and in the towns of the Stewartry. In earlier times the Scottish street must have been gay and colourful indeed – in salutary contrast to the drab vistas of grey rough-cast and brown pebble-dash so monotonously popular between the wars.

Since the war, white and coloured cement washes have been increasingly used, but although lime wash is admittedly less durable, there is good reason to prefer it as a finish on lime harling or pointed stonework. It is physically and chemically akin to lime harling, and shares the porosity which, as we have previously remarked, is a valuable property in a harling. Lime does not contain salts injurious to stone, and compared to cement it is much more tolerant of colour pigments and is itself of a more luminous whiteness.

Lime wash is made by slaking quicklime with water and adding animal or vegetable fat or oil while the slaked lime is still hot. What happens is that some of the oil or fat reacts with the alkaline lime to form an insoluble calcium soap, and the rest of the oil is emulsified by this soap and binds the mixture together. A typical formula for the mixture (in quantities sufficient for a small house) is ten pounds of tallow or a gallon of linseed oil to one hundredweight of dry quick-lime. In some present-day versions, used motor sump oil is substituted for the tallow or linseed oil – probably because it costs nothing. Such mineral oils do not react at all with lime, and if these mixtures are successful – and there is some evidence to show that they are – it can only be that the oil is temporarily emulsified by vigorous stirring. Some traditional recipes include a little common salt, but it is difficult to see what good this does, and it may be that the idea was carried over, in vaguely hopeful imitation, from the domestic process of soap-making in which salt was used in conjunction with tallow and caustic soda.

After steeping for at least sixteen hours, the wash should be thinned with water to a creamy consistency and applied in two coats with a brush. The wall must be thoroughly cleaned, and the first coat should be made rather thinner so that it may be well worked into crevices and rough parts.

Pure lime wash of this kind tends to become half-transparent when wetted by rain. This can be got over by making up a wash containing white pigments of greater opacity – for example, a mixture containing two parts pure lime wash as above, two parts whiting, and one part zinc oxide. Colour pigments added to lime wash should be the so-called 'earth' colours, firstly because they are stable in lime (hence their extensive use in fresco painting), and secondly because they go well with the colours of building materials and landscape. Mixed with lime wash, these earths give rise to a wide range of pleasant colours – reds, yellows, and browns, vivid or quiet, pale or dark. Colour, as we have said, can be exciting, but it must be chosen with the greatest care to go with the slates, tiles, stone, and the adjacent buildings and trees.

6. Roofs

In making a survey of the roof, the first thing to look into is the condition of its framing. Timbers may be failing because they are too light for their purpose or are inadequately braced or strutted, or because they have been weakened by rot or by insect attack. Sometimes defects may be obvious, but even when the roof looks quite sound you must examine it carefully for any incipient defects or bad construction which might give rise to trouble later.

If the roof has been neglected it is very probably leaking, and you can expect to find some rotting of the timbers. The most likely place is where the timbers bear on the outer walls, for here the water tends to collect and any wood resting on or embedded in the stonework becomes thoroughly damp. In a roof covered in sheet lead or asphalt the chances of dry rot occurring are quite high, but in the better-ventilated pitched roof in slate or tile any rot is more likely to be of a less virulent sort. Dry rot requires a fairly elaborate treatment which we have outlined earlier, but wet rot may be dealt with more summarily by cutting out the infected wood and treating all adjacent wood with a preservative.

You may find that the roof has been attacked by woodworm. The 'worm' is usually the larva of the Common Furniture Beetle (the much-publicised Death Watch Beetle does not occur in Scotland). Unless the attack is very severe, the loss of strength in the main timbers is unlikely to be serious, for in a traditional roof such timbers are usually stout enough to afford a considerable loss of body without risk of failure. Lighter pieces such as sarking boards or ceiling branders are more vulnerable, and may have to be replaced. But whether or not the immediate damage is material, the risk of continued or renewed attack must be guarded against. If no fresh dust falls out of the bore-holes when the wood is tapped with a hammer, it is probable that the attack has ceased, but it is still advisable to scrape away any soft timber and to give the whole roof a thorough brushing with an insecticide. If there is the slightest evidence of active infestation, a much fuller treatment – summarised later in the section on Joinerwork – will be necessary.

Individual roof members may be strengthened by fishing new pieces of timber or metal straps to them, or by introducing extra bracing. Weak joints may be made good by binding them with iron. If you find that an entire couple is in bad condition, the simplest and cheapest course may be to take the load off it altogether by erecting a new couple close alongside.

Frequently it is found that a roof has been weakened by the removal of an internal partition which was originally designed to strut it. In the case of a simple roof of coupled rafters and ties, the only visible effect may be some local sagging in the ties, but if the rafters have been strutted from the ties they too will show signs of overloading. The remedy is to put back the original support, either in the form of a new load-bearing partition or of a beam spanning between convenient cross partitions (*fig.* 15). Should there be objections to showing such a beam on the ceiling, it can be fixed as a binder above the level of the ceiling ties, with metal hangers dropping from it to support them. A third device, which obviates any need for supporting partitions and therefore leaves you free to plan rooms without regard to the roof, is to make the roof, or part of it, into what is called a 'double roof' by trussing every fourth couple and running purlins and binders to lend additional support to the intermediate rafters and ties.

Sometimes there is a general sagging in the roof which cannot be put down to unsound timbers or lack of supports, and you are driven to conclude that the timbers are simply too light for the loads they have to carry. The probability is that at some time in its history the original covering of the roof has been replaced by one of a heavier type. When you consider that the dead weight of a slated roof is half as much again

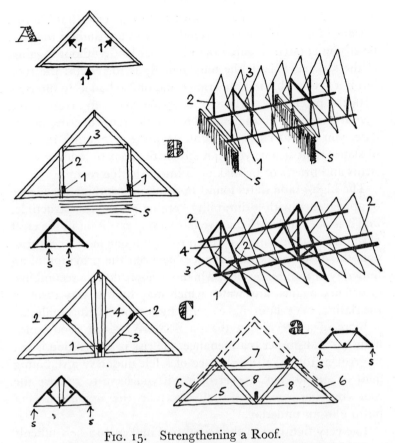

FIG. 15.   Strengthening a Roof.

A: Sagging rafters and ties need support at the points marked (1)
B: Ties may be supported by hangers fixed to beams or binders (1)
   spanning between load-bearing partitions (s), and the rafters by
   struts (2) rising from the binders. A collar (3) increases the
   rigidity of the roof.
C: In the absence of convenient partitions, the same support can
   be given by making a 'double' roof. A binder (1) for the ties,
   and purlins (2) for the rafters, can be carried on trusses made by
   adding struts (3) and ties (4) to every fourth couple. Alternatively, to obviate any extra load on existing timbers, independent frames (a) of struts (6, 7) and ties (5, 8) may be inserted in
   between existing couples to support the binder and purlins.
The small diagrams show the principles of the constructions, the
compression members being marked in heavy lines.

as that of a pantiled roof, it is only to be expected that if a roof designed for pantiles is re-covered in slates the timbers may not be strong enough to carry the increased load without sagging. If the sagging is bad, the only remedy is to rebuild the roof, but if it is tolerable in appearance and not so bad as to interfere with the proper lie of the roof covering, you can arrest it and save the roof. If you intend to renew the roof covering in any case, you should choose a lighter type (e.g. pantiles in place of slates), but if not, you can stiffen the roof by adding extra struts and braces or by making it into a double roof.

The high-grade slates found in Scotland combine excellence of appearance with a durability verging on the indestructible, and it is not surprising that we have a fine tradition in the craft of slating. Comparing a modern roof with one of two centuries ago, the only significant advance has been the provision of an underlay of bituminous felt, which we now add as a second line of defence against any water which may find its way through the slating. Yet slates make such a tight roof that this underlay is more of a precaution than a necessity: given good work-manship and proper maintenance, the risk of infiltration is not so great as to make the absence of a felt underlay a damning fault in an old roof. Nevertheless, if you have to remove the roof covering you should always take the opportunity of putting in an underlay.

The very tightness of the slated roof makes it rather difficult to repair. Slates can of course be replaced, but since this can-not be done without disturbing adjacent slates and weakening their fastenings, repair does not quite reinstate the roof in the sense of making it as good as it ever was: eventually further repair is not worth while and it becomes necessary to strip and re-slate. Some roofs have been repaired so often that the sarking boards are no longer able to hold nails, and the roof is said to be 'nail-sick'. The proper cure is to lay new sarking; a cheaper but less satisfactory expedient is to fix a system of battens on top of the old sarking to carry the slates.

When re-slating, you should make use of the old slates as far as possible and supplement them with second-hand ones. Most modern slates are cut so thin and smooth that they will neither lie snugly with the older rougher sort nor give the same characteristic boldness of texture. English and Welsh slates, excellent though many of them are, do not blend with Scottish materials, and the cheaper Welsh slates are so thin that the roof looks poor and meagre and has a relatively short life. The traditional practice of grading the size of slate between eaves and ridge should be followed, for it is technically sound and greatly improves the look of the roof. In some districts – notably in the Stewartry – this grading is very marked indeed, to the extent of becoming a distinctive and most attractive feature of the local buildings.

Early roofs were finished with a stone capping at the ridge. In reconstruction, this is one place where good cast stone can be used to save money without serious loss of appearance. The separate lengths of capping should be shaped to key together, each joint should be underlaid with a strip of damp-course, and the angle of the capping should be considerably steeper than that of the roof-slope, to leave space for a generous mortar bedding and to give a firm, neat finish to the skyline. In the eighteenth century, stone ridges gave place to lead-work, and this metal, which suits the dark Scottish slates, should be used in preference to copper, aluminium, or zinc. The use of tiled ridges on slated roofs was a Victorian innovation, and is to be deprecated. Dark-coloured tiles are perhaps passable, but red ones are deplorable.

In finishing slate-work at skews and chimney-stacks the old practice was to carry the slates into a raggle in the stonework and to seal the joint with a fillet of mortar (*fig.* 16). This works quite well if the slates are given a good tilt up to the stone and are taken deep into a generous raggle. The mortar fillet must be small and well tucked in under the stone, for large fillets are as unreliable as they are ugly: they abound with shrinkage cracks

and are very liable to damage by frost. Where there is no
possibility of good overhanging cover to such joints, it is much

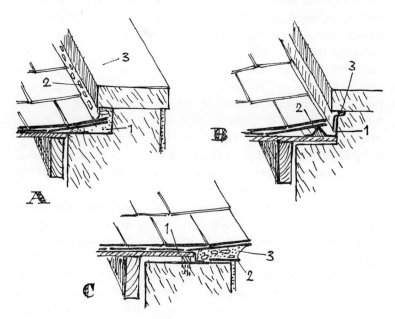

FIG. 16.   Skews in Slated Roofs.

A: Section showing slates tilted in a mortar bed (1) and jointed to
   the skew cope (3) by a mortar fillet (2) packed with small stones
   or pieces of slate to prevent shrinkage cracking.
B: Slates are tilted on a wood fillet (2), and a lead or copper gutter
   (1) is worked over the tilting fillet on the one side and covered on
   the other by a flashing (3) raggled under the cope.
C: Section showing a skew finished in slates: the wood sarking (1)
   stops short of the gable, and the slates at the skew are bedded to
   a cement mortar fillet (3) resting on a creasing course of slates (2)
   bedded on the gable stonework.

better to use metal flashings and soakers in the normal manner.
    The perfect way to treat a valley between intersecting roof-
slopes is to finish it with slates alone, as either a 'swept' or a
'laced' valley (*fig.* 17). Such junctions are not only technically
excellent but impart a wonderful feeling of unity to the roof.

The swept valley is the finer but more expensive of the two, for the slates have to be shaped to work round the curve. In the laced valley no special cutting is needed, though it too calls for skill on the part of the slater. The next best method, in point of

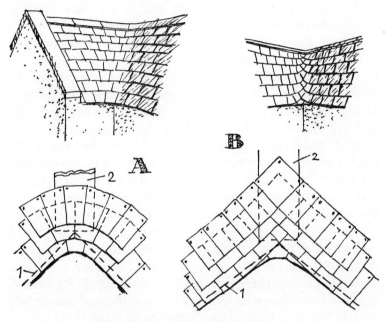

FIG. 17.   Valleys in Slated Roofs.

A: A swept or circled valley. The walls are shown dotted in true plan (1). The valley is formed by working tapered slates round the angle over a broad valley-board (2), every second course being in slate-and-a-half widths.

B: A laced valley, the plan being in the plane of the valley slope. The slates are not specially cut but are kept tight at the heads so that they sweep up in curves to the junction of the roofs.

appearance, is the 'secret' gutter in lead, but it is rather easily blocked by leaves and other debris, and the uglier 'open' gutter is the more practical choice. If it is used it should be kept as narrow as is consistent with freedom from blockage.

In the east of Scotland, pantiles have been in use for centuries. Properly hung, they make a durable and watertight roof, and the colour and rhythmic pattern of the snugly fitting tiles is most attractive. A good example is to be prized and preserved, for unfortunately most old roofs have suffered from neglect and careless maintenance and few survive in their pristine condition. In some cases the sagging of roof timbers may have upset the lie of the tiles; but usually the mischief has been caused by using tiles of a slightly different sett to replace cracked originals, and since the fit is not perfect the roof is not watertight. The jobbing tiler's answer to the problem is external pointing, which is not only ugly but inefficient and pernicious, for the mortar cracks away from the tiles, water is drawn into the open joint, and salts contained in the mortar leach out and cause decay in the tiles. Internal pointing is unobjectionable and may be successful if the roof is in a sheltered situation. But in all other cases the only satisfactory answer is to lift and re-hang the tiles on a bituminous felt underlay (*fig.* 18). This should be laid in lapped courses along the roof and nailed to the rafters before new tiling battens are fixed; to keep the battens clear of any water trickling down it, the felt should be allowed to sag slightly between the rafters. Rigid sarking is not strictly necessary, but it makes the roof stouter and greatly improves thermal insulation, particularly if you use an insulation board or foil-backed plaster sarking. Tiling battens are commonly nailed directly above the felted sarking, but it is better practice to interpose counter-battens running down the slope, to leave a space for the free passage of water down the felt.

Pantiles were traditionally red, though occasionally a dark, almost black tile was used. Modern aberrations such as green or glazed or 'antique' tiles should be avoided like the plague. Hand-made tiles old or new (they are still manufactured) should be used in preference to machine-made ones, which lack the liveliness of texture of the more traditional article. Old tiles vary considerably in size and curve (which is not

surprising, since they were imported or manufactured in small
quantities) and you must be careful not to mix different lots
on the one slope: should it prove impossible to get enough tiles
of any one sort to do the whole roof, one lot may be used for
one slope and a second for the other. You cannot over-
emphasise the importance of perfect fit: pantiles must match
in profile and be hung at the proper gauge with their shoulders

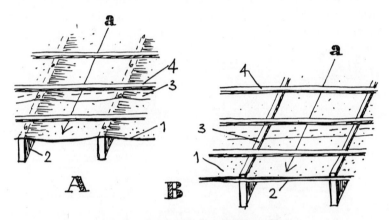

FIG. 18.   Battening for Tiles or Slates.

A: A roof without sarking. The under-slating felt (1) is laid across
   the rafters (2) with a generous overlap (3) at joinings. It is
   allowed to sag slightly between rafters so that a water-way (a)
   is formed under and entirely clear of the tiling battens (4).
B: A roof with rigid sarking. The felt (1) is laid over the sarking
   (2) and the water-way (a) is formed by raising the tiling battens
   (4) on counterbattens (3) running down the slope.

butting closely together. These are points which you must
impress upon the tradesman and be prepared to insist upon,
for all too many modern tilers, whose experience of old pantiles
has been limited to ill-patched roofs, start off with the conviction that it is not possible to make a sound job with them.
In this frame of mind they regard existing tiles as expendable,
and will think nothing of introducing a few foreigners from a
job lot of tiles lying in their yard.

Scottish practice differs from English in using slates instead of plain tiles as the undercloak of the eaves of a pantiled roof. From this develops an interesting variant form of eaves in which the first few courses of the roof are formed in slates instead of tiles (*fig.* 19). This tight slated eaves is much less liable to lift in high winds and presents a surface on which the concentrated rush of storm-water down the hollows of the pantiles is distributed before it is discharged from the roof. Besides being highly functional, this band of slatework makes the finish of the roof clear and firm, and shows an agreeable contrast in colour and

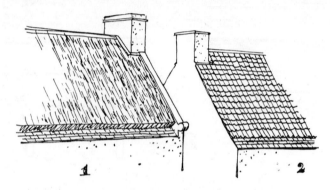

FIG. 19. A characteristic use of slates at the eaves of (1) thatched and (2) pantiled roofs.

texture. This device might well be used to eke out the old tiles when too few of them survive to restore a roof which was originally pantiled to the eaves.

Roofing in stone slates is a very ancient form, which has been carried on for centuries with little change in style or method. Its cost, and the cost of the comparatively massive framing required to support it, are considerable, yet the craft still exists and restoration is still possible. The substitution of a slate or tile roof for an original stone one is to be deprecated most strongly: the stone roofs in Angus, for example, are a very important part of the building tradition there.

Thatch was once very common in Scotland, even in burghs, though it seems that it never achieved the success it did in England, where a less severe climate, an abundance of good materials, and a comparative absence of competition from other inexpensive roof-coverings fostered a craft of great skill and virtuosity. In Scotland, the use of thatch declined rapidly when slate and pantile became plentiful and cheap enough to compete with it, and today the craft is on the verge of extinction: it is probably the literal truth to say that there are but two or three properly skilled tradesmen left in the country. Yet as we show later in the history of a typical case, it is still possible to thatch a house with Scottish reed at a cost which compares well with that of any other roof-covering. Supplies of material are limited – machine-threshed straw is useless for the purpose – but what is available is of such a quality that maintenance should not exceed that required by most other roofing materials. Fire insurance may be heavier, but against that the high thermal insulation provided – at no extra capital cost – by the thatch itself should result in an appreciable saving in the running cost of heating. As with stone slates, it is scarcely to be expected that this excellent and comely roofing will be used in new building, and it is the more earnestly to be hoped that restorers will be found to preserve the few theikit biggins left to us.

7. Fireplaces and Chimney-stacks

The principles of the efficient design of fireplaces and flues were first laid down in 1796 by Sir Benjamin Thompson, Count Rumford, in his essay *Of Chimney Fireplaces*. In the Advertisement to his essay, Rumford relates how his acquaintance Sir John Sinclair (the great Improver and the compiler of the first *Statistical Account of Scotland*), knowing of Rumford's success in treating upwards of five hundred defective fireplaces in London, persuaded the Lord Provost and Magistrates of Edinburgh 'to vote a sum of money to defray the expenses of a bricklayer, who is to be sent them for the purpose of establishing the same plan in that city', and how it was while instructing this missionary tradesman that Rumford conceived the idea of publishing his work in full detail and without taking out any patent, that all and sundry might freely put his discoveries into practice without need of further instruction. Despite this gesture, Rumford's teaching was given scant attention in this country, and for another century and a half Britons continued to be plagued by inefficient fireplaces and smoky flues. In recent years rationing and the rising price of coal, together with warnings about the approaching exhaustion of our coal resources, awakened us to the urgent need to use it less wastefully, and at long last Rumford's ideas have come into their own as the recognised basis of the design of new improved fireplaces. If the improvement of an old fireplace sometimes poses a difficult aesthetic problem, there is a certain compensation in the fact that in thus 'modernising' we are in reality applying an eighteenth-century science which the eighteenth century itself chose to ignore.

The leading points of Rumford's theory are these: the fireplace opening should be kept as low as possible (two feet high or less); the fire-back should be about one-third as wide as the opening at the front, the sides of the fireplace being splayed to eliminate side pockets of cooler air, and the depth from front to back should be sufficient to prevent the fire smoking because of draughts across the opening; the fire-back immediately above the fire should be sloped forward to augment the output of radiant heat; the 'throat' or entry to the chimney should be perpendicularly above the centre of the fire, and should be six to eight inches in vertical depth, while its width from front to back should be restricted to four inches or less to speed up the flow of gases by aerodynamic effect; the bottom of the lintel over the fire should be streamlined to lead in room air without

PLATE 11

HAMILTON DOWER HOUSE
PRESTONPANS

Restored by the National Trust for Scotland. Note the fluent, unified effect produced by swept valleys in the roofs (cf. p. 78).

The summary treatment of the eaves of the tower roof (*below*) is typical of the Scottish tradition. Its sculptural precision of form had been blurred by the addition of rain-water gutters (*above*).

PLATE 12. KIRKLEA COTTAGE, BLAIRLOGIE

The extension on the left (*above*) was built with materials
salvaged from ruined buildings nearby.
For Case History, see p. 117.

turbulence; and, finally, above the throat there should be a
flat smoke-shelf to baffle down-draught, and a small smoke

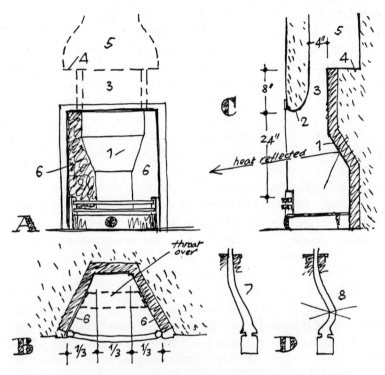

FIG. 20.   Count Rumford's Principles.

A, B, C: Elevation, plan and section of a fireplace, showing (1)
sloped fire-back, (2) stream-lined lintel to lead room-air into the
flue without turbulence, (3) deep and narrow throat centrally
above grate, (4) flat smoke-shelf and (5) small smoke-chamber,
(6) splayed sides and decided narrowing of the fireplace towards
the back.

D: The flue should run from smoke-chamber to chimney-can as
straightly as possible (7), any unavoidable bends being slow
and smoothly turned. The sharp kink (8) often introduced is
more likely to cause than to prevent down-draught.

chamber smoothly gathered into the flue. The optimum width
of throat is about two inches, but unless it is made adjust-

G

able this will be too narrow for effective chimney-cleaning.

With some ingenuity it is possible to remodel or Rumfordise old fireplaces, utilising old grates such as the charming Carron cast iron hob grate or the early Victorian register grate. This treatment is most satisfactory in point of aesthetics, is not expensive, and will raise efficiency quite considerably: but there is no denying that if you want to get maximum efficiency you must instal modern appliances with devices for positive draught control, secondary heating by convected air, and so on. How successful you are in marrying the new to the old depends partly on the degree of formality of the room (for the casual cottage room is more tolerant of change than the sophisticated town house drawing-room), and partly on the care you exercise in choosing the appliance and in designing the surround. The range and choice of appliances is widening year by year, and you should go to some trouble to find the simplest and lightest design available. By setting the fireplace in a panel of tiles – not modern lustred tiles, but period ones – you can effect a transition between the new unit and an old mantelpiece. If it is not an old one adapted for the purpose, the surround should be a genuine piece of unforced modern design using materials of the same type and character as those of the existing building. Most fireplaces in cottages have surrounds of dressed stonework, and some simple ways of treating them are suggested in the sketch (*fig.* 21). The phony ingleneuk, the quasi-gothic stonework, the prefabricated unit of moulded tiles, and the English facing brick are all wildly out of place.

Old flues must be examined for defects. You may find the stones near the base of the flue calcined by heat, or the parging or mortar lining of the flue broken away, allowing smoke to percolate into the stonework. It may be sufficient to renew the parging, but if extensive repairs are needed you will be well advised to insert fire-clay flue-linings. A flue serving a slow combustion stove or cooker is very liable to damage by condensation and should always be lined. Flues should be as straight as possible: the deliberate kink almost automatically provided by many architects and most builders, in the belief that it will check down-draught, in fact does nothing but hinder the upward flow of gases and increase the chance of a blow-down. The best insurances against down-draught are the

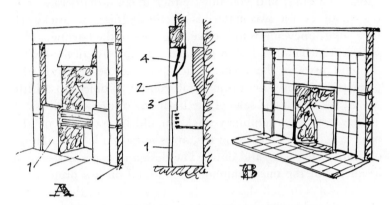

FIG. 21. Improvement of Cottage Fireplaces.

A: Sketch and section of a high narrow fireplace with existing built hobs (1) and barred grate retained. Some improvement may be effected by infilling above the hobs (2), addition of a fire-back (3) and a double-skinned hood in sheet metal (4).

B: The greatest possible efficiency may be obtained by installing a good modern fireplace within the stone opening, set in a panel of tiles, whitewashed cement plaster or other finish. The base of the flue must be modified (on the lines of Fig. 20). Any tiling should be of traditional type – plain quarries, or glazed decorated tiles, and the mantelpiece a plain board.

narrow throat and flat smoke-shelf advocated by Rumford, and a flue with the least possible obstruction of the upward flow.

In a house built in ashlar there is really no alternative but to accept the expense of rebuilding any decayed chimney-stacks in ashlar too; but if the walls are in rubble a tolerable job can be made with brick, provided it is done with discretion. The chimney-stacks are an important part of the external elevation, and if rebuilt in brick they must be generous in size and approximate to proportions more typical of stonework than of brick-work. The common eighteen-inch brick stack will not do – and in any case its thin walls render the flues cold, damp, and sluggish. Brickwork has a flat straight surface which even when harled does not blend easily with the characteristic surface of rubble masonry, and you must either make a deliberate con-trast between the two materials or else disguise the brickwork by a slight unevenness in the backing coat of the harling. This sounds unprincipled, but in the larger perspective of the design the end justifies the means, and it would be straining the principle of expression of materials too far to object to a little honest faking for the sake of the harmony of the whole.

New copings to chimney-stacks should be modelled on the originals, if available, or on examples found on local buildings of similar character and date. The design of copes varies with locality, but the most common type found on less pretentious houses is a thin slab showing about two inches of thickness on face and projecting not more than an inch and a half over the faces of the stack. Chimney pots were not used in the seven-teenth century, and in a reconstruction of this date the coping should be flaunched or sloped upwards from its edges and the flues finished with short lengths of fire-clay drain-pipe standing about two inches above the flaunching. By the eighteenth century, chimney pots had become an integral part of the design – though not such large and ornamented features as they later became in the nineteenth century – and replace-ments should be of moderate length, neither lanky nor stumpy, buff in colour, and simple in form.

8. Floors

Apart from its other considerable merits, the solid type of ground floor has special usefulness in reconstruction work. Since it does not rest on the walls, such a floor can be laid with the least possible disturbance of the existing structure, and the same independence makes it easy to damp-proof where it abuts damp walls. Since it needs no ventilation, you are spared the expense and hazard of cutting through thick stone walls to form air inlets, and when, as often happens, you are looking for inches to maintain or increase the ceiling heights of ground-floor rooms, the fact that you can lay a solid floor near or even below ground level assumes great importance. For these reasons the solid floor is often to be preferred to the suspended timber floor. It is frequently objected that a solid floor is cold, but this belief is founded on a confusion. Warmth or coldness to the touch depends on the floor finish alone – any floor will be cold to the touch if it is finished with a good thermal con-ductor, such as stone or clay tile, but will not feel cold if it is surfaced with a poor conductor, such as wood or cork. The degree of surface coldness is no measure of the thermal insula-tion of the floor construction as a whole. In fact the heat-loss through the usual type of hung timber floor with ventilated under-space is twice the loss through a solid floor of the simplest form; and the solid floor is the only one which can, without great elaboration, reach the standards of thermal insulation recommended for ground floors.

Unless it is positively damp-proof, an existing solid floor cannot be left as it is (*fig.* 22). If it is sound and well bedded down, you can lay a damp-proof membrane directly on top of it and cover with a new finish. The alternative is to scrap the existing work and to form a new concrete sub-floor with a damp-course. In either case the essential point is that the membrane must be continuous and must be properly joined to any damp-proofing of walls and partitions. The almost equally important matter of the correct position of thermal insulation in floors is dealt with in the section on damp prevention.

The wide and bewildering range of finishes for solid floors includes various types of jointless flooring, quarry tiles, thermo-plastic, rubber, cork or linoleum sheet or tiles, woodblocks,

prefabricated wood parquet, and wood boarding. Each has its
merits and limitations, and choice cannot be made until the

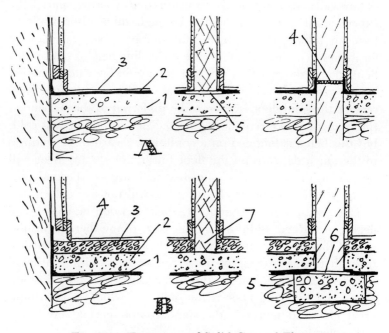

FIG. 22.   Treatment of Solid Ground Floors.

A: If an existing floor (1) is unprotected against damp, a continuous
   solum damp-course (2) must be laid down, bonded to any new
   damp-courses formed in existing partitions (4) and to felt damp-
   courses (5) laid under all new partitions. To prevent condensation trouble (cf: Fig. 7) the finish (3) should be of material with
   a high thermal resistance.

B: In a new floor, the damp-course (1) is better laid under the floor
   slab (2), and if this is topped by an insulating screed of vermiculite concrete (3) the floor finish (4) may be of any kind. The
   solum damp-course must be continually bonded to the damp-
   course (6) placed under any load-bearing partition (which should
   pass through the floor slab to rest on its own foundation (5)).
   Non-load-bearing walls (7) are simply built off the slab and are
   protected by the main damp-course underneath it.

various characteristics – appearance, resilience, resistance to
abrasion or water or grease, ease of maintenance and so on –

have been considered in relation to the varying needs of different rooms. There is not space to discuss the legion of proprietary finishes, but wood boarding deserves mention – if

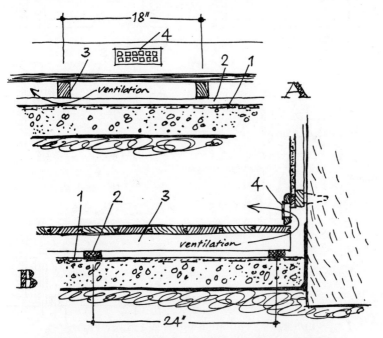

FIG. 23. Timber Boarded Finish to a Concrete Floor.

A, B: Sections along and across the floor construction: After the top of the concrete slab has been made smooth and level (1), a set of $2'' \times \frac{3}{4}''$ bearers (2), well treated with preservative, is laid down and crossed by $2'' \times 1\frac{1}{2}''$ counterbearers (3) which receive the floor boarding. Any rubbish must be thoroughly cleared out so that air may circulate freely under and between the counter-bearers and up behind the skirting, where ventilation is provided by holes (4) cut through the skirting near each corner of the room and at intervals of about six feet along each wall. The holes are covered by metal frets.

only because it is often overlooked. A boarded floor laid on a system of bearers resting on a concrete sub-floor combines most of the good qualities of a joisted floor with the virtues of a solid

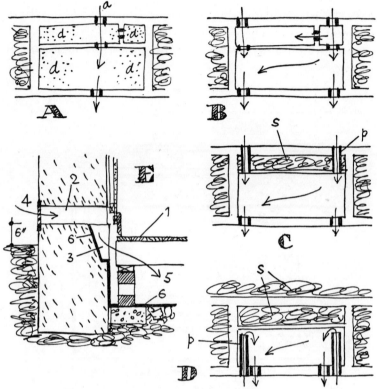

FIG. 24.   Ventilation under a Timber Floor.

A: The plan shows a typical under-building, with fresh-air inlets
marked by heavy lines. The single inlets shown will set up a
cross-ventilation (a) but many pockets of dead or stagnant air (d)
will be left.

B: A double system of inlets eliminates all dead pockets.

C: If part of the floor is solid, cross-ventilation under the suspended
part can be maintained by laying pipes (p) through the solid
sections (s).

D: If the outside air can be reached from one side of the house only,
the necessary circulation can be set up by fitting a second pair
of inlets with pipes to duct air to the back of the space.

E: The section shows how a fresh-air inlet is formed when the floor
(1) is at or below ground-level. The inlet (2) is at the normal
level, but is cranked down at its inner end (3) so that air may pass
freely from the grating (4) to the under-floor space (5). The damp-
course (6) should be carried up at all points to a level at least
six inches above the ground.

floor. It fits in with a traditional building, and in selected soft-wood costs in all about the same as, say, the better grades of thermoplastic tiles on a cement screed. The sketch (*fig.* 23) shows details of the construction including the necessary ventilation through the skirting.

The first question to be asked about a joisted floor is whether it is safe from damp. The timbers can become damp by direct contact with walls or – in the case of ground floors – by absorbing moisture from the air in the space under the floor: therefore no such floor can be considered safe unless it is separated from walls and ground by damp-courses and ventilated spaces. It is folly to retain an existing timber ground floor unless you have examined the space underneath it. If the earth is in contact with the joists it must be excavated until there is a space of at least three inches clear below the joists, and the ground must be levelled, blinded with sand, and sealed with a layer of pitch-oil or other damp-proof membrane. If the space under the floor is not ventilated, air ducts must be cut through the outside walls so that all pockets of dead air are eliminated by cross ventilation. If you cannot draw air from both sides of the house, the necessary through draught can be created by ducting some of the air in pipes, as shown in the sketch (*fig.* 24).

Joist-ends, wall-plates, and other timber solidly embedded in the walls are an open invitation to wet or dry rot and must be attended to. (Timbers with end, sides, and top free and ventilated are not quite such bad risks, but even these must be suspect if there is any possibility of damp in the surface on which they rest.) The best thing to do in the case of embedded joists is to provide a new support so that the joists may be cut off clear of the wall altogether (*fig.* 25). The old joist ends must be removed completely and the freshly-cut timber treated with preservative. In a ground floor, the new support can be a honeycomb brick wall built a few inches clear of the stone wall. In upper floors, a steel angle, or a timber bearer supported on galvanised iron corbel pins, may be used. Yet if you are satis-

fied that the wall-holds of an upper floor are reasonably dry you
may leave the joists as they are, provided you rake out the mortar which is packed round them and check any latent rot by
pouring preservative over the joist-ends. When fitting any new
joists or repairing rotted ends by scarfing on new timber, you

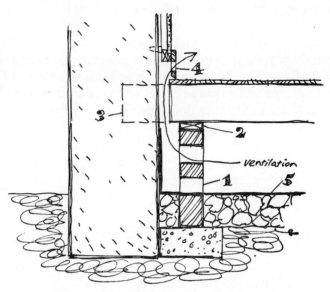

FIG. 25.   Isolating a Timber Ground Floor from a Damp Wall.
A new wall (1) in honey-comb brickwork is built to carry the floor-
joists. The new wall-plate (2) is separated from the wall by a felt
damp-course. The ends of the joists (3) are cut off and removed
from the old wall-holds. The under-floor space must be ventilated –
failing all else, by skirting-board grilles (4). The ground below
and the inside face of the stone wall is sealed by a damp-course (5).

should enlarge the wall-holds to allow air to circulate freely,
treat the timber with preservative, and wrap the end of it with a
piece of bitumen damp-course. If you are forming a new upper
floor at a level different from that of the original one, the best
form of support is the metal or timber corbel already mentioned,
or one of the variant concealed types shown in the sketch (*fig.*
26). By fixing the floor in this way, you obviate the need for

cutting new wall-holds in the stone, which apart from anything
else may seriously weaken the wall.

Sagging joists are often found in old houses. The timbers
may have been too light in the first place, or have been over-
loaded by new partitions above them, or have lost some intermediate support they once had, or the wood may have been

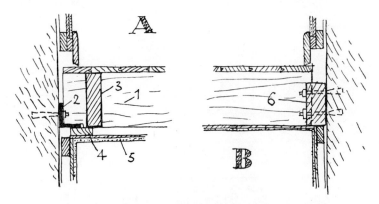

FIG. 26.   Fixing an Upper Floor to Stone Walls.

A: The floor joists (1) rest in the bosom of a steel angle (2) bolted
to the wall, and are fixed in position by a row of short pieces or
dwangs (3) wedged between them. The steel should be painted
with bitumen paint, and the joist-ends treated with preservative.
The plaster ceiling (5) is best fixed on branders (4) running across
and below the joists.

B: Alternatively, the joists may be housed into and spiked to a thick
timber bearer (6) bolted to the wall. The bearer should be treated
with preservative and painted with bitumen paint on the face
which is in contact with the stone, and the bolts should be staggered.

weakened by rough usage, rot, or insect borers. The straightforward answer is to strut the joists with some kind of intermediate support. If the plan allows it, a new partition may
be built underneath, or a timber beam carried across the
ceiling. If for reasons of style or for lack of head-room an exposed beam is undesirable, the joists may be notched on the
underside to receive a steel tee beam running above ceiling
level (*fig.* 27). Should the span be long, this steel beam will be

quite large and much of the substance of the joists will have to be cut away to accommodate it. This in turn will weaken the joists in their secondary (but often very necessary) function of tying the outside walls of the house, and to compensate for this loss of strength the two parts of every second or third joist should be joined together by a strong iron dog passing under or over the

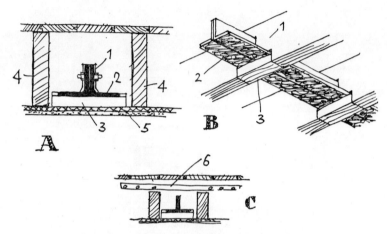

FIG. 27. Beam concealed within a Floor.

A, B: Section and sketch from below. The joists (1) are notched out to take a steel beam formed of two angles bolted back to back. To provide nailing surface for ceiling lath (5) the beam is set high enough to allow a nailing piece (3) to be jammed and nailed into the notch. Dwanging (4) should be added to hold the joists rigidly in position.

C: If the floor is being relied upon to stiffen the walls it rests on, the weakened part of the joist should be strengthened by an iron strap (6).

steel beam. In certain circumstances you can make use of an upper-floor partition to brace a weak floor (*fig.* 28). If such a partition runs across the way of the joists and rests at either end on a load-bearing wall, it can be framed in timber to act as a deep girder spanning between these walls, and the floor can be supported by fixing the joists with hangers to the bottom of the partition.

It has been remarked earlier that a joisted ground floor, cooled as it is by the through currents of air in the under-floor space, is far from satisfactory as a heat insulator. A big improvement can be made – quite cheaply – by plating the floor with insulation board before laying the timber boarding, though to challenge the performance of a solid ground floor a

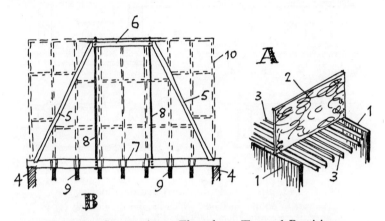

FIG. 28.   Supporting a Floor by a Trussed Partition.

A: The sketch shows the principle of the construction: the partition (2) can be made to act as a deep, stiff beam spanning between supporting walls (1), and so to support floor joists (3) attached by hangers to its lower edge.

B: Details of the construction: (4) Supporting walls; (5) main struts; (6) head strut; (7) main tie; (8) ties formed by steel rods bolted top and bottom. The floor joists (9) are attached by metal hangers to the main tie. The rest of the framing (10) is arranged in the usual way to suit plaster lathing.

much more elaborate construction of mineral wool resting on fibreboard carried on fillets and dwangs between the joists is required.

Deafening of upper floors is desirable in a self-contained house, and essential if the building is divided into flats. If the floorboards can be lifted, the process is the same as for new building. The old-fashioned pugging (a weak mix of ashes and sand with lime or plaster) is the most effective deafening,

but you must first of all check that the joists are strong enough
to carry the extra weight. A lighter form combines a smaller
amount of pugging with a floor floated on an insulating quilt.
Compared with an undeafened floor this treatment raises the

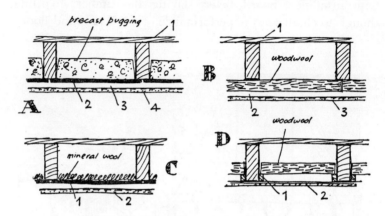

FIG. 29.   Deafening an Existing Floor.

In contrast to normal methods, which require the flooring (1) to
be lifted, these constructions are worked from below.

A: Pugging consisting of ashes and shavings bonded with plaster is
pre-cast upon strips of plaster-board (2) which are then hoisted
and nailed to joists. The ceiling is then brandered (3) and finished
in metal/wood lath and plaster.

B: Wood-wool slabs are nailed to the joists, and the ceiling is brandered (with long fixing nails passing through the wood-wool to
the joists) and finished in metal/wood lath and plaster.

C: A variant of (A) for use when joists are not strong enough to take
the weight of plaster pugging. The mineral wool will not be as
effective as a heavy material, and the boarding (1) should be as
thick as possible and the ceiling (2) metal/wood lathed.

D: Wood-wool slabs are slipped on to wood fillets (1) nailed to
joists, and the ceiling (2) is fixed direct to joists in cases where
little loss of head-room can be afforded.

insulation more than halfway towards the standard represented
by the pugging method: it is adequate perhaps for houses, but
not for flats. When the floorboards are not being lifted, less
orthodox methods, such as those illustrated in the sketches (*fig.*
29), must be improvised. Although they have not been sub-

jected to scientific tests there seems to be no reason why they should not give results comparable to those of more usual forms of deafening. A point to note is that recent research has shown that deafening is more effective when fixed rigidly to the joists – contrary to the accepted practice of resting it loosely on fillets. It has also been found that sound transmission is markedly reduced when the ceiling plaster is based on wood or metal lath instead of plaster lath.

If it is not too badly worn, a boarded floor may be brought to a new surface by machine-sanding, and if the old floor is in a good yellow pine it is worth going to much trouble to save it, for new timber of the same quality will be hard to come by. Square-edged boards may be sanded-off so long as their reduced thickness is not less than the minimum required for stiffness; but when boards are tongued and grooved a certain body of timber must be left above the grooves, for otherwise long slivers of wood will split off along the joints.

The laying of a new timber floor should be put off as long as possible after the plasterwork is finished. In the days of lime plaster there had to be a pause of some weeks after plastering to allow it to harden, during which time much of the moisture in walls and plaster was able to dry out; but today, with modern quick-setting plasters, it is possible – and indeed usual – for the joiner to start work as soon as plastering is finished. Although his timber may be properly dry when he bring it into the house, it immediately begins to absorb moisture from the cold damp building, swelling and twisting in the process. Later, when the house is occupied, heated, and dried out, ugly shrinkages inevitably appear. Much of the unsatisfactory new woodwork which is blamed on 'the badly-seasoned timber you get nowadays' is in fact caused by this hasty procedure in building. Ideally, no joinerwork should be fixed until the building is as warm and as dry as it will be when occupied. In practice we have to be content with something less than this, but if you give the building plenty of ventilation and some temporary heating after plastering, leaving it for at least a fortnight before allowing the joiner to start, you will reap a rich reward in the final state of floors and woodwork.

The finish of a timber floor should sink into the surface so that the two seem to be one, and the natural grain and character of the wood is enhanced. Wax polish is unrivalled in the silky finish it gives to a floor. Contrary to popular belief it is not waterproof, and before polishing the freshly-sanded floor it should be sealed with a solution of gold size in turpentine or with another preparation sold for the purpose. The depth and sheen of a waxed finish increases with repeated polishing, but there are now on the market synthetic varnishes which, though they cannot match the subtle gleam of a waxed finish, give a high gloss from the beginning. Such varnishes should be applied in a succession of thin coats, each rubbed down with fine sandpaper. At first the look of the floor may be spoilt by the varnish lifting the grain of the wood slightly, but after a while this roughness wears off. Synthetic varnishes give a hard, durable, and waterproof surface, but there is the drawback that marks caused by really rough usage are difficult to make good without cleaning off to the bare wood and renewing the treatment.

9. Joinerwork

In an earlier section we emphasised that as much of the old material as possible should be incorporated in the restored building, and this applies to nothing more emphatically than it does to joinery finishings – mouldings, doors, windows, panelling, and the like. These are the parts of the building which are seen and handled most by the people who live in it, and for this reason they do much to fix its character. The difficulty is that they are also the things which suffer most from neglect and mutilation, and you will be lucky indeed if you find the woodwork of a house so well preserved that it is easily restored.

More often you will find some of it in fair condition, but much of it defaced or damaged and in need of extensive repair or complete replacement. Since replacement – as we shall see – has its problems, you should hesitate before discarding any material which is not beyond all hope of redemption: even if it must be patched or pieced out in ways which cannot be concealed, it will bring a quality to the job which no new material can give.

In making replacements, modern stock materials of so-called 'traditional' type are in the main useless for your purpose. Most of them are coarse and debased copies of eighteenth-century prototypes, which, by contrast, were distinguished by a lightness and delicacy amounting to elegance, even when they were made by unsophisticated craftsmen. It is of course possible to have timber specially run to match the old work, though the process is more or less expensive depending on the quantity and type of material required. It is usually feasible to make moulded facings and windows in this way; but when it comes to more complex articles (such as panelled doors) the cost may be prohibitive, and it is better to look for second-hand material of the right period. Plenty of such doors are to be found in demolition contractors' yards, though it requires a personal visit to pick out those of suitable style and size. The amount by which you can reduce an old door in size to fit an existing doorway depends upon the amount of wood covering the tenons at the joints, but usually a maximum of half an inch can safely be taken off each side member or stile, and rather more off the bottom rail. Should the door be too small for the opening, an eke-piece could be planted on one or both stiles, but it is often better to reduce the opening by planting a plate on the ingo of the door frame, making the facings wider to cover it. If you cannot find suitable second-hand material, you should design new woodwork in a simple modern fashion: the mixture of old and new, if carried out in a straightforward manner, can be spirited and quite satisfying.

H

The panelled door reached the peak of its elegance in the eighteenth century, and good examples are to be found not only in fine town houses but in cottages of modest pretensions. Such doors are distinguished by their good proportions and by the way they are made: the mouldings are not separate pieces of wood planted on after the door has been framed up, but are worked on the solid of the framing members them-selves. The panels are sometimes plain but more often fielded – that is, raised in the middle. In external doors, the panels are often thick enough to come flush with the face of the framing, the joint round the panel being marked with a sunk beading. In the seventeenth century, two-panel doors were common, but in the eighteenth century there were usually six. The four-panel door typical of Victorian and later times is poorly pro-portioned by comparison and looks top-heavy.

The boarded or clad doors of the period differ from modern ones in being made in very wide boards – sometimes only two or three in the width of the door. This broad cladding has a much better appearance than the narrow V-jointed lining commonly used today, which looks mean and busy. The simplest form of clad door is made of vertical boards clench-nailed to three horizontal back-bars, with or without diagonal bracing (*fig.* 30). Unless it is soundly built in well-seasoned timber – as most old doors were – it is liable to twist or to sag from the hinges. In the case of an outside door the bars on the back are unobtrusive, but on internal doors their effect is decidedly unsophisticated and suits only the simplest cottage interiors. Another form of clad door is constructed on the same principle as modern plywood, having no framework, but an outer cladding of vertical boards clench-nailed to an inner one of horizontal boards. The familiar nail-studded doors of medie-val and Jacobean times were cross-clad in this way (hence the characteristic nail-patterns), but by the eighteenth century the heavy planking and great iron nails gave place to thin boards and concealed nailing, and the form acquired considerable elegance, with delicate sunk beading at the joints of the vertical boards. The total thickness of some examples is as little as three-

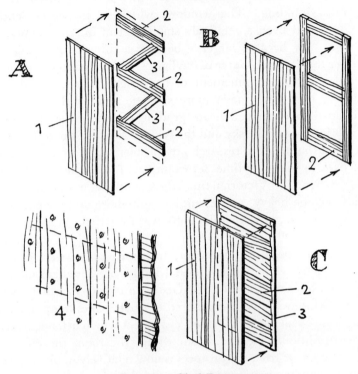

Fig. 30.   Clad Doors.

A: The simplest form, consisting of cladding (1) nailed to back-bars (2) with or without braces (3).

B: A bound door, consisting of cladding (1) nailed to a proper frame (2) with mortice and tenon joints.

C: A cross-clad door, consisting essentially of an outer cladding (1) of vertical boards clench-nailed to an inner cladding (2) of horizontal boards. The inner boards are sometimes dove-tailed into narrow edging strips (3) to prevent end-wood from showing. The characteristic nail pattern (4) is sometimes made decorative by use of large-headed nails.

quarters of an inch, yet the construction is inherently so strong and stable that they remain perfect after two hundred years.

By the eighteenth century the sliding sash-and-case window had virtually superseded the earlier casement type, being more in keeping with the Palladian style which was now influencing Scottish building. The window, which in the seventeenth century had been a relatively small part of interior domestic design, now became larger – became a thing to look out of rather than a mere source of daylight – and increasing attention was paid to the refinement of its design. The astragals or glazing bars were made more slender, and mouldings were designed to effect a delicate grading of tone-values between the brightness of the sky and the relative shade of the room. (It is a fact that modern research into problems of glare has had to go back to Georgian times for examples of well-considered window design.) In Victorian times these subtleties were lost: astragals became heavy, and mouldings grandiose and coarse, and the ideal of a glare-free silhouette was forgotten. With the invention of rolled glass the small panes formerly dictated by blown glass began to disappear, and entire sashes were glazed in one pane. The single-paned window has practical merits, but you have only to look at a Georgian terrace in which some of the windows have been altered to single panes to appreciate the loss of scale and the 'blind eye' effect which attends its use in a traditional façade. From within the room the effect is equally great: true, the prospect is now relatively unobstructed, but it may be questioned whether this is to be preferred to the formal relationship between interior and exterior which was expressed by the delicate pattern of the eighteenth-century astragals. An appreciation of these points should restrain you from using the coarse stock mouldings of today for repairs or replacements, and from doing violence to the harmony of the building by introducing designs which are foreign to the tradition and based on a radically different conception.

Judged by our standards of ventilation and convenience, many old sash-and-case windows are unsatisfactory in that one sash may be fixed and the moving sash not counterbalanced.

To instal sash weights is expensive and may often be impossible for lack of room for the weight-boxes: it is better to counterbalance the window with patent spring balances, which can be fitted without much trouble. Such balances are especially useful in the construction of multiple windows, for since bulky weight-boxes are eliminated the mullions can be made very slender, to the great improvement of the appearance of the window.

Fungal attack on timber has been discussed in a previous section. Insect attack is less deadly – certainly as far as the structure is concerned: but for all that it can do serious damage to the building and to your furniture. The characteristic sign is the appearance of numerous small holes in the surface of the wood, accompanied by fine dust falling out of the borings. These borings are made by the larvae of beetles which feed on the wood itself and gradually destroy its substance. If the attack reaches an advanced stage the timber becomes quite soft and crumbling as if it were rotten – indeed severe insect damage is frequently mistaken for rot by people who do not appreciate the significance of the adjacent flight-holes.

In Scotland, the pest is usually the Common Furniture Beetle *Anobium punctatum*, a reddish-brown insect about an eighth of an inch long which appears in the summer months and lays its white eggs in crevices in the woodwork. The eggs hatch, and the larvae or so-called woodworm eat and tunnel through the timber. In the following spring they settle down to pupate in chambers close under the surface of the wood, and in summer emerge as beetles, flying or crawling away to spread the infestation further. Eradication is a simple but often lengthy and tedious job. Sterilisation by heat is the best remedy, but it is difficult to apply to most joinerwork and you will probably have to resort to insecticides – paraffin, turpentine, or more lethal proprietary insecticides (the last should always be used for polished woodwork). The liquid must be well worked into the wood and if you can squirt it into the flight-holes so much the better. The best time for treatment is during spring and summer when the pupae are lying near the surface. Not one but several applications will be needed in the first season, spaced at fortnightly intervals, and it is probable that it will take two or more seasons' work to eradicate the pest completely.

If old woodwork has been covered by so many layers of paint that the mouldings are blurred and the surface poor, it must be stripped. This is a niggling and tedious process; and since it is only too easy to damage the wood by scorching with the blow-lamp or nicking with the scraper or overdoing the sandpapering, the work should be entrusted to no one but a person who can see the end from the beginning and who will plod on patiently and carefully, neither scamping nor rushing the work. If you intend to repaint the wood, burning-off is permissible; but if it is to be left finished in its natural colour the blowlamp must on no account be used. After dry-scraping to remove the top layers of paint, you should soften the undercoats with a paint solvent. Caustic soda is very effective and imparts a good colour to the stripped wood, but it is unpleasant to work with – staining the finger-nails and burning holes in clothes. Since it may attack the glue in framed joints and saponify any new wax or paint finishes, it must be completely removed from the wood by thorough washing. If the work has to be done *in situ* it is better to use the more expensive but less messy and unpleasant proprietary paint-removers. If you want to treat stripped surfaces for woodworm, you should remember that most insecticides are oil-based and will therefore darken the wood: if a pale finish is wanted, carbon bisulphide is a suitable alternative though it is dangerously inflammable and has a pungent smell.

Stripped woodwork may be finished by waxing with a prepared beeswax polish or with a solution of beeswax in turpentine. This must be applied very thinly in several coats, each well rubbed in (any polish advertised as 'requiring no rubbing' will almost certainly contain a varnish and give a less attractive finish). The final coat should be burnished with a brush. Waxing is not waterproof and horizontal surfaces are liable to become marked by spilt water, damp vases, etc. These marks can be removed by camphorated oil and much hard rubbing: the alternative is to make the surface water-proof before waxing by rubbing in a thin coat of colourless oil sealer.

10. Ironmongery and Lighting Fittings

In a restored house the use of even a few genuinely old metal fittings can have an effect out of all proportion to their size and number. Fittings which we have tended to regard as museum pieces take on a new dimension when, in daily use, we discover that they are practical and efficient. Familiarity in this case is likely to breed nothing but increased respect for the mechanical ingenuity of their design: tangible experience gives a new insight into the craft, indeed the minds, of their makers. All this may explain the peculiar interest they lend to an old house. Yet it may well be that having gathered together as many old pieces as you can find in the building itself or in half-forgotten corners of joiners' shops or in sale-rooms, you will not have enough, and will have to add some new fittings. Their choice requires much thought and care, for most of the things you will be offered will be of the wrong kind.

In old Scottish ironwork, for example, we find the same purity and economy of design, the same functionalism and touches of homely fancy which mark our traditional architecture. At the very opposite pole is the modern mass-produced ironmongery which sets out to appear antique. Its pseudo-handwrought finish cannot deceive anyone with an eye for craftsmanship, and its forms are for the most part poor if not bogus – mere coy camouflage of modern fittings. Even when an ancient model is followed it is usually one of English medie-

val provenance and a particularly florid example, far removed
in spirit from the simplicity of traditional Scottish work. Much
of the faking is ludicrous – for example the strap-hinge which
is not a hinge at all but merely an ornament fixed on the face
(often the wrong face) of a door which is in fact hung on
separate butt hinges. The avoidance of such obviously bogus
stuff is easy: it is not so easy to separate the good from the bad
in hand-wrought ironwork which professes to follow tradition,
because the traditional method of manufacture tends to be-
glamourise us and to confuse the issue. The fact that an article
has been forged on an anvil by the hammer of a technically
expert craftsman cannot in itself save it from being just as bogus
as the worst of the mass-produced articles: equally, the fact
that an article of traditional design has been stamped out by
the thousand does not automatically condemn it as bogus.
It is necessary to distinguish between the replica (which in its
fidelity may catch some of the spirit of the original), the
approximate copy (which misses the life of the original and has
no flicker of its own), and the functional article which is only
incidentally formed in a traditional idiom. One practical guide
is to look for simplicity and functionalism above all things:
neither will rob the article of traditional feeling. The jobbing
blacksmith may very well be able to give you what you want;
if you go to a more sophisticated craftsman be wary, for special-
isation in hand-wrought work tends to vitiate design by a self-
conscious determination to be traditional.

To have things made to order is naturally not the cheapest
way of completing your ironmongery. A special fitting will cost
more than one chosen from stock: in the case of a simple thing
such as a hinge, a little more; in the case of a complex thing
such as a latch, much more. It may be that you will, for the
sake of economy, have to make do with a mixed lot – some
old fittings, some new ones hand-made, and the rest standard
stock fittings. Such a compromise may sound disappointing,
but – possibly because it is unashamedly matter-of-fact – it may

be more successful than an elaborate scheme of matched fittings, which can so easily become self-conscious in its very consistency.

The usual hinge for clad or boarded doors is the T-hinge. The form which seems to have been most common in Scotland is plain and unadorned but for a simple fish-tail worked at the end of the strap of the hinge. The Lancashire hinge, still shown in some catalogues, is a close cousin to it, and though it has a bulbous end instead of the fish-tail only a fanatical purist would object to its use. The cheaper standard steel T-hinge has no particular grace about it but at the same time it is inoffensive and looks quite well if its shiny black japanned finish is replaced by paint or berlin black. Yet for a few shillings extra you can have a hinge of traditional pattern made up for you by a blacksmith, and it is well worth while going to this expense for the hinges of principal doors at least.

The corresponding door fastening is the sneck or thumblatch with bow handles. Old types varied in form: some had back-plates, some had not; some were plain, some were embellished. What ornament there was derived very directly from the nature of the metal and the smith's tools. Handles might be drawn out to swell in the hand-grip and taper at the ends, or be forged into a faceted section with a slight central ridge; handle-ends might be palmed out in little trefoils, or the rim of a back-plate might be frilled with punch marks. By comparison the common modern version of the sneck, sold under the name of Suffolk latch, is so crude and uncouth that it can hardly be recommended: if you need new latches the extra cost of having them made will be money well spent. The one place where the simple sneck is not fully satisfactory is at a principal entrance door, where you need a lock. You can of course fit your sneck and a separate deadlock, or you can combine latch and lock by using a standard weighted lock which, having bow handles and thumb lever, will go quite well with snecks on adjacent doors. Cupboard doors need not be fitted with snecks, and it is cheaper to fit a standard roller latch in combination with a bow handle made to match the sneck handles.

In days when screws were neither common nor cheap, T-hinges and snecks were riveted to the doors by wrought-iron nails driven right through and clenched over. It would seem pedantic to do this today, with screws at hand to do the job as

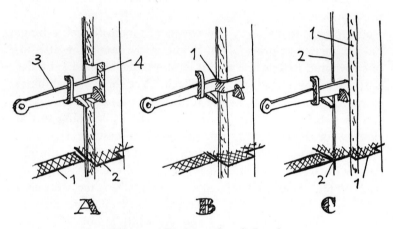

FIG. 31.   Fitting a Sneck Latch.

A: When the door and facing (shown in plan at (1) and (2)) are in the usual relationship, the fitting of a plain sneck (3) involves the cutting of a notch (4) in the facing.

B: Notching of the facing can be avoided by using a cranked sneck (1).

C: As an alternative to method A, the facing (1) may be set back about half- or three-quarters-of-an-inch from the edge of the door standard (2).

well if not better, but counter-sunk slot-head screws lack the decorative appearance of the old nail-head and it is better to use square-headed coach screws.

Door facings almost flush with the inside edge of the door frame in the standard modern fashion, need to be notched to accommodate the keeper of a sneck or a rim lock (*fig.* 31). A much neater way is to make room for the keepers by changing the style of the facings, setting them back about half an inch from the edge of the door frame. If you do this, the door frame itself will have to be dressed and jointed with special care, for more of it will be visible than if the facings had been fixed in the normal position.

The eighteenth-century panelled door was furnished with a rim lock or latch in brass, generally moulded in a severe architectural style. Such old locks differ markedly from modern ones in their proportions: the lock-cases are larger and the handles smaller than their modern counterparts. For this reason it is difficult to find new locks that will go with old ones, and if you cannot collect enough old rim locks to do your job you will probably have to fall back on the mortice type. But before ordering a mortice lock you must make sure that your door is thick enough to house it. Many eighteenth-century doors are so thin that only a rim lock will serve.

Most modern door handles look too big and clumsy on an old rim lock and are generally difficult to fix satisfactorily: the original would have been either a little drop handle or a small knob, round, oval, or faceted. But with a mortice lock there is no objection on the score of size to an otherwise suitable modern handle. Should the pattern you want be available only in antique bronze finish you need not be deterred, for if the handle is of good quality it will have a brass body and the dull finish can be easily removed with metal polish. The bronzed surface may be labour-saving, but in appearance it cannot compete with the bright winking of the polished metal, which needs no more cleaning than an occasional rub with a dry duster. The rest of the furniture – the keyhole escutcheon and the finger-plate – will have to match. The finger-plate is advisable if your door is stripped and waxed. If you are not a stickler for consistency in period, you may turn to Victorian painted china furniture, which can look very pleasant and is now reproduced in a great variety of designs.

The ubiquitous electric door-bell has deprived our front doors of the knockers and tirling-pins which used to be their chief ornament. The door-bell and its related system of room-bells was a necessity in houses with remote servants' quarters, but social change, particularly in the last thirty years, has resulted in the withering-away of the system until now only the front door-bell remains. It seems probable that the use of electric bells in our compactly small houses of today is a subconscious carry-over from the villa'd past rather than a considered rejection of the older devices on the ground of efficiency. The fact is that, provided they are properly designed and placed, the knocker and the pin are, either of them, perfectly adequate in most small houses. Old knockers, unlike some modern ones, are massive enough to give an unmistakable summons which fully justifies their ancient and sombre name of deid-nail, while the tirling-pin or risp produces a sound which is remarkably penetrating and easy to distinguish among other domestic noises. The important point about both devices is that they depend upon the resonance of the door itself to amplify the sound they make. They are therefore relatively ineffective unless the door is shut, and if fitted to an outer door which you habitually leave open when you are at home they may prove more ornamental than useful. The sound can also be muffled by intervening doors or by travelling round corners, and if your kitchen and living-room are remote from the front door you had better fit an electric bell. Although there is no objection to a neat modern push-button, it is an easy matter to adapt an old brass draw-bell to operate an electric bell circuit.

Early knockers were made of wrought iron and the hammer was separate from the striking-plate, which was often a nail with a large flat head. Later, when cast iron and brass came into use, both parts of the knocker were mounted on the one back-plate and the whole was often elaborated in a bold and fanciful design. These later knockers are appropriate to the finer panelled doors, while the wrought iron variety is best used for more primitive types. The tirling-pin is generally found in association with the sneck-latch, and is often (with typical economy) combined with the outer bow handle of the sneck. Given the common principle of a metal ring rubbing against a serrated edge, the variety of forms is legion (*fig.* 32). Some are very simple but others attain a fair degree of sophistication: for example, the serrations may be provided by the spiral fluting of a miniature baroque column. Tirling-pins, in contrast to

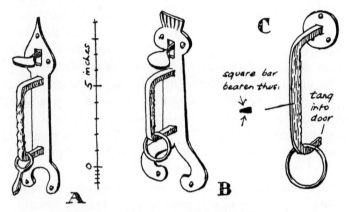

FIG. 32. Examples of Tirling Pins.

A, B: Tirling pins combined with the outer part of a sneck latch. The necessary risp is supplied by twisting the rod (A) or by serrating its inner face (B). The simple thistle ornament in (B) is produced by dinting with the chisel.

C: A type which also serves as a bow-handle. The bottom part of the bow is angled upwards to keep the ring away from the door.

knockers, are now something of a rarity, but there are one or two craftsmen in Scotland who still turn them out – or you can have a good example copied by a blacksmith.

Window fittings should be neat and unobtrusive in design, and made of metal to match your door furniture. Small knobs in painted china can be obtained for shutters if you are using similar furniture on doors. Shutters have such practical value – insulating you most effectively against the egress of heat and the ingress of draughts and burglars – that you may want to put them into working order. The traditional fastening was an iron bar which clamped across the back of the shutters – a highly effective device, for it cannot be opened from outside except by cutting a hole through the shutters. The bar was quite light and flat. Sometimes it was hung from a swivel fixing at one side of the window, dangling in the shutter recess when not in use. When the shutters were closed it was swung across and its free end fastened by a cleat or by an iron turn-button on a stalk passing through a slotted hole in the bar. Another method was to pivot the bar on the back of one shutter near the meeting edge so that it could be rotated like a giant turn-button to engage in cleats at either side of the shutters.

The installation of electric light in an old house is a clean break with the past of candles and oil-lamps, and nothing is more futile than an electric system which attempts to disguise itself as something else. There is a place – as we shall note below – for some incidental use of old lamps and lanterns adapted to electricity, but only within a scheme which is designed to make sensible and efficient use of the modern means of lighting. Nevertheless, it is possible to be kind or unkind to a building in the way you light it and in the fittings you use, and only by careful thought will you arrive at a scheme which not only satisfies working requirements but enhances the appearance of the house.

In the cottages we are considering the original illumination was typically from a low level – the table top, the mantel-shelf, the dresser – and you will find that your rooms will look much better if you avoid ceiling fittings. This is especially the case if the rooms are low: for a fitting so little above eye-level is very obtrusive by day, and by night it shows up every imperfection of the ceiling surface and produces considerable glare and discomfort. Even in service rooms, such as the kitchen or the bathroom, top light is not a necessity: indeed, if carefully placed (for example, immediately above a cooker or sink, or beside a mirror) lighting by wall-units is a positive advantage. It is true that an installation of low-level lighting points, requiring as it does at least two points in each room, tends to be more expensive than one which relies on ceiling points for primary illumination; yet it is being increasingly recognised that such a system is the right one for domestic purposes in any kind of house, and it is certainly the most successful in old houses of the cottage type.

Wall-bracket lights should be wired directly into boxes in the wall and controlled by a switch at the door (if you can afford the acme of convenience, the control can be of two-way type with one switch at the door and another at or near the fitting). Other lamps of portable types should be catered for by a generous provision of sockets, either controlled in the same way or integrated with a general ring-main system of 13 amp switch-sockets. Where the lamp is likely to be on a mantel-shelf or on top of a built-in fitment, you should obviate the need for unsightly trailing flex by placing a socket immediately behind the lamp position. Switch-covers and socket-plates should be of a substantial pattern and are best of plain design, though we would make an exception in favour of decorated china switch-covers if you are using similar door furniture.

In choosing fittings, the type to be avoided at all costs is the fake candle (complete with eternal drip of wax) or similar attempt to disguise your illuminant as anything but electricity. Nor should you indulge in Gothic lanterns, medieval wrought-iron switch-plates or other whigmaleeries which, even if they could be supposed to have any merit, certainly do not have that of being in period with a house which was built two centuries after the style they are derived from went out. You will be much better served by simple, straightforward modern fittings – not those with hard shapes (which are designed for clear-cut modern interiors) but those which, though unequivocally electrical, give something of the quiet and mellow effect which characterised the oil-lamp.

Within this general scheme of modern illumination it is possible, if you are so minded, to add atmosphere and interest to the house by introducing old lamps adapted to electricity, or specially made fittings which, without offending common-sense, copy old forms of lamp housing. Many Victorian oil-lamps, whose conversion to electricity is a matter of ingenuity rather than expense, are highly decorative and make excellent table-lamps. In antique shops they sell at fancy prices, but they can still be found and bought quite cheaply in back-street junk shops. For outside lights most modern fittings are sternly utilitarian; some are nothing short of ugly, but even those which are so well designed as to fit into an old setting can scarcely be said to enhance it. Here is an opportunity to use an old fitting or a new one modelled on some good example – not an olde worlde medieval watchman's handlamp dangling on a bracket, but a good sonsie yard lamp of the type which may still be seen at the vehicle entry of some elderly building or on the platforms of a few moribund railway stations in the country. Glazed on three sides (the fourth side being attached to the wall) and surmounted by a stumpy cowled chimney, they are efficient and often attain considerable if plain elegance. The main work in adapting them is to ensure that the lamp is watertight and so protected against corrosion. Lanterns made of copper can be burnished and varnished; if made of iron they should be scraped clean and galvanised after the adaptation has been done, and painted dull black.

PLATE 13. NAIRN'S BUILDINGS, LAIGH FENWICK

The original eighteenth-century façade was restored by opening a blocked-up window, which can be seen under the harling in the picture above. The white harled walls give full value to the scrolled skew-putts and other dressed stonework. *For Case History, see* p. 122.

PLATE 14. OXHILL, KIPPEN

The view before reconstruction (*above*) is from the north-east,
and shows the outside stair which is now the main entrance to
the house. The view below is from the south-east and includes
the same gable. *For Case History, see* p. 127.

3

Case Histories

The case histories which follow illustrate many of the points made in this book. The buildings are all typical, and the notes, without going into great detail, show how such derelict properties can be brought up to modern standards and turned into pleasant and useful houses.

The statements of cost are not intended to give more than a general notion of the cost of this kind of work. Direct comparison between the various jobs is made impossible by differences in the date of pricing, the extent of the work, the amount let to contract, and in the standard of finishes, services, and equipment provided. In each case the cost of works (exclusive of purchase price, fees, and legal expenses) has been expressed as a rate per square foot of gross area within external walls. During the decade in which these jobs were done the corresponding cost of new brick-built houses of similar size and standards ranged from 45s. upwards to 55s. per square foot.

I. Cottage at Blairlogie, Stirling

The restorer first saw this cottage in 1940. It was empty, the last occupants having apparently been a party of soldiers. The factors said that the cottage was condemned: they understood that the County Council intended to demolish it, in order to widen a corner in the road – a dead end, giving access to twenty houses, and then used by about as many vehicles in any one day. Accordingly the factors did not regard the building as saleable, but were willing to transfer ownership of it by feuing

I

the plot in which it stood for £5 per annum. On being approached the County Council agreed that the road-widening
was only a post-war possibility, and consented to the restoration
of the building, provided it was brought up to reasonable
habitation standards.

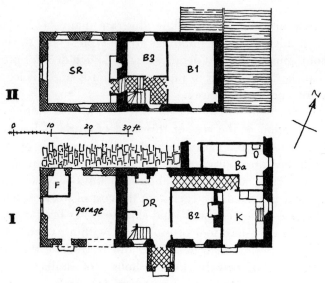

FIG. 33.   Kirklea Cottage, Blairlogie.
New work is shown hatched.

The cottage had originally been the end one of a row of four
– probably the last to be built, since it was by far the most
substantial, and the only one of two storeys. The other three
had been mud-mortared and thatched: a lintel above the
doorway of one was dated 1758. They were already in ruins.
At the other end the building had originally been free-standing,
being on a corner site, but a large lean-to wash-house had been
built on, which joined it to another single-storey cottage behind
and at a right angle to it.
The main building, containing four rooms, was more or less

wind and watertight. The lean-to addition was derelict, the roof having partially collapsed. The walls were of boulder rubble (many of the boulders being whin) with dressed sandstone window and door surrounds. There was no damp-proof course. The roofs of both main building and lean-to were pantiled, without sarking. The ground floor was mainly much-patched concrete, but in one room there was a wooden floor. There was no sanitation, and only one cold tap, in the wash-house.

Owing to wartime building restrictions the reconstruction was carried out piecemeal, and much that was skimped or left undone at first has had to be re-done since. The owner did not employ an architect, and in many ways this reconstruction has been an object lesson in how not to set about the business. Initial work consisted of making a kitchen and a bathroom out of the lean-to. The roof was replaced in its original position, but the ceiling was raised eighteen inches, so there is a slight coom at one side of both rooms. Part of this area had a rock floor three feet above the rest of the house – the story in the village was that it had been a bake-house but there was nothing to substantiate that. Cutting away the rock proved expensive and laborious: there seemed also to be some danger that it might weaken the gable of the neighbouring cottage, so the bathroom floor remains six inches higher than the rest of the house. A new brick wall between kitchen and bathroom was, most unwisely, built off the old concrete floor without a damp-proof course. This mistake is only one of several which have since had to be rectified.

A free-standing cooking and water-heating stove was substituted for the old wash-house boiler, using the same flue. The existing main water pipe was used, though its point of entry has since been changed. In the main building the only initial alterations were the removal of a kitchen range in what is now the dining-room; the conversion of the single window in that ill-lit room to a french window; the removal of the broken

ceiling in the downstairs sitting-room to leave the joists exposed
(a make-shift means of improving ceiling height); the removal
of a tiny box-room beside the top of the stairs to form a small
open landing lit by what had been the box-room window immediately above the front porch. Electricity was installed, and
a good deal of broken plaster patched. The flooring of the
landing and one room upstairs had to be completely renewed.
Two of the original window sashes had to be replaced, one or
two of the others required minor patching, and all of them had
to be hung in new cases with sash-weights. Outside, the ground
at the back had to be taken down about two feet – it had previously come up to window-sill level. A septic tank was built
about a hundred yards from the house.

These alterations, together with the replacement of broken
gutters and rone pipes, painting of external woodwork, and
minor repairs, cost about £400.

A year or two of living in the house, however, showed that
they had been inadequate. The main roof leaked in heavy
rain or snow, as did the new roof over the kitchen and bathroom,
which had ill-advisedly been replaced in its original form of
pantiles simply hung on battens. After a couple of winters
both roofs were sarked, felted, and battened, and the tiles rehung. In the new roof this represented an expenditure of about
£20 more than it would have cost had it been sarked and felted
at its initial replacement. In the main roof several badly
wormed couples had to be replaced.

The old concrete floors also proved quite unsatisfactory.
Damp came up through them, and their unevenness made them
difficult to clean. So they were covered with a magnesite
flooring compound on a bitumastic base, which has proved
completely resistant to rising damp and given a pleasant-look-
ing and easily cleaned surface, though being a plain colour it
shows footmarks much more readily than a marled finish would
have done. It was laid (again through lack of an architect's
guidance) with no thermal insulation between it and the old

floor, which means that the new floor is kept cold by the damp concrete under it, and the damp earth under that, and is therefore more liable to condensation moisture in humid weather than it would have been had a layer of insulation been introduced. It has been found necessary to treat all the ground-floor walls for rising damp with two coats of waterproof cement skimmed with lime plaster to a height of about two feet on external walls; brick partitions, old and new, have had a damp-proof course inserted. In the case of the ground-floor sitting-room the old wooden floor proved unsatisfactory – on occasions of exceptionally prolonged rainfall water would ooze up between the floorboards. (Although the two-inch bearers were resting on damp earth not one of them was completely rotten, yet it appeared to be the original floor, which means that they had survived such bad conditions for over 150 years.) The earth was excavated to a depth of eighteen inches, covered with concrete, and the whole tanked with bitumen, rising to a height of two feet above floor level. The joists supporting the new wooden floor rest on brick piers, each with an additional damp-proof course. As the ground outside is only a couple of inches below floor level, and a solid-floored passage behind the room made through ventilation impossible, four ventilating openings were cut in the front wall, sloping downward through it. Two end when they come through the wall, the other two are piped to the back of the room.

Since the war the cottage has been extended by the addition, at the opposite gable from the lean-to, of a double garage and a room (the largest in the house) above it. The extension is built in rubble stone, the garage doorways being formed with cart-shed arches from a nearby derelict farm steading. The extension follows exactly the roof and window lines of the original house, and increases the frontage by about half.

To gain entry to the new room an opening was made in the original gable wall and an entirely new stair, branching two ways from its half-landing, was constructed. The original lobby was thrown into the dining-room – mainly for the sake of light from the staircase window. Since this would have left the front door opening directly into the room, a stone porch with inner and outer doors was built to replace the old open shelter-porch. Daylighting in the kitchen has also been much improved by substituting for the original solid back door one with a glazed upper half which is hinged, so that it can open as a window.

The cost of these latter improvements and additions has been about £1,500; with the original £400 the total outlay has been under £2,000, or 23s. per square foot of internal area (including garage) at 1940-53 prices. At least £100 of that could have been saved if the original reconstruction work had been more radical, avoiding the necessity of re-doing so much of it. Had the whole reconstruction been done in one operation instead of piecemeal, the saving would have been greater. As it is, a pleasant cottage of five rooms, kitchen, bathroom, and double garage, with every modern convenience, has cost little more than half the price of a comparable new house.

2. House at Laigh Fenwick, Ayrshire

The would-be restorer, in search of a suitable building, spent a week in 1943 visiting villages in Ayrshire and Renfrewshire within twenty-five miles of Glasgow. Although handicapped by having to rely on public transport (except for one day on a bicycle borrowed from a helpful minister) he found a score of empty cottages in varying stages of dereliction which would have amply repaid reconstruction; but most of them would only have made three- or four-roomed houses, whereas he required six rooms and kitchen. By the end of the week he had rather rashly bought two buildings, both condemned, one in Eaglesham (price £100) and the other in Laigh Fenwick (price £150).

On applying to the Renfrewshire County Council for permission to reconstruct the house in Eaglesham he was met with a flat refusal. The building line of the street, he was informed, was to be set back about ten feet, to which end about forty houses were to be demolished after the war. His suggestion that it would be more practical to move the roadway, since there was nothing but the enormous village green on the other side of it, was regarded as frivolous. Outraged by this almost

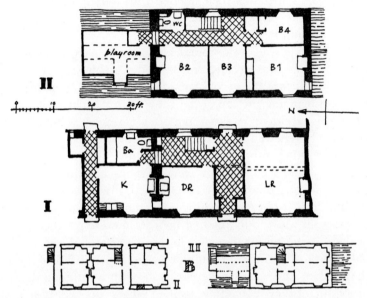

FIG. 34.   Nairn's Buildings, Laigh Fenwick.
B: Plans (to half-scale) before reconstruction.

unbelievable example of official stupidity and intransigence, he reported it to the Department of Health for Scotland, with the highly satisfactory result that the entire street, together with the corresponding street on the other side of the village green, was subsequently listed as an entity in the highest degree worthy of preservation.

By that time, however, he had received permission from Ayr County Council to recondition his property in Laigh Fenwick, a late eighteenth-century two-storey house in harled rubble, with a slate roof. The street elevation is simple but well proportioned, with no special features except scrolled and embellished skew-putts. It is joined on either side to single-storey cottages. Half of one of these cottages went with the house, the other half having been taken in to a reconstructed cottage beyond it. While the main building may originally have been a single house, it was then divided into four flats, each consisting of one large and one small room. The most recent occupants had been squatters.

The outside walls were sound for the most part, though one chimney-head was unsafe, and indeed was blown down in a storm just before the reconstruction was started, breaking the roof and bringing the top of the gable with it. The roof, apart from this accident, was in reasonable repair, having been completely renewed some twenty years previously.

The existing subdivision proved quite unsuitable for re-planning, and as the floors were in poor condition and no internal feature of any interest remained, it was decided to gut the building. Almost everything was removed, including plaster on external walls; only the first-floor joists were retained, most of them being sound though a few had to be reinforced. The old square tiles of the ground floor were kept for future use in the garden, and a new concrete floor (with a bitumen damp-proof membrane extending twelve inches up the inside of external walls) was laid throughout. In the two public rooms this was covered with thin beech blocks; in the hall and passage with marled red thermoplastic tiles.

The ground floor of the half cottage was made into the kitchen premises and bathroom. The floor level was a foot higher than that of the main house, and as sinking it meant going below the foundations, it was left at its original height with two steps up to it in the access passage, for which an opening had to be cut through the gable wall of the main house. The new concrete floor was covered in the kitchen with a magnesite and rubber compound, in the bathroom with cork tiles.

As there is no access road to the garden at the back of the house, a through passage was formed beyond the kitchen, leading from the so-called back door (which is in the front of the half cottage) to a literal back door into the garden. This allows coal, bicycles, or even a wheelbarrow to be taken through the house.

The only external alteration to the street elevation was in fact a restoration. Under the harling could be seen the outline of a built-up window, which was opened again. In each gable wall of the main building a small window was inserted above the adjoining roof to meet daylighting requirements in two of the bedrooms. These windows are obviously an improvement to the two rooms, and externally they add interest to the otherwise blank areas of gable wall rising above the neighbouring roofs. At the back of the house one window on the ground floor was converted into a french window, giving access to the garden from the entrance hall, and providing a very attractive vista from the front door. Another partially blocked window was restored. The only other external alteration at the back was the provision of a flat dormer window in the roof of the half cottage, to give headroom and light to a new access through the gable wall to the room above the new kitchen and bathroom. This awkwardly coom-ceiled room, formed in an attic space, had previously been approached by a very narrow stairway which was now scrapped, and a new party wall was built up to the roof to provide adequate deafening and fire-stop between the two halves of this divided cottage.

Upstairs in the main building two double and two single bedrooms were formed with built-in wardrobes. Plumbing was kept compact by placing the lavatory at the end nearest the kitchen and bathroom. New bedroom doors were made of traditional boarded construction, with thumb-latches wrought by a local smith. For the public rooms downstairs old six-panelled doors in yellow pine were bought for five shillings each in a demolition contractor's yard. Stripped and waxed they looked notably pleasant, and painted china handles and finger plates, though not strictly in period, enhanced them. Since the hall and sitting-room extend from front to back of the house, it was necessary to provide some intermediate support for the first-floor joists, and a heavy pine cross-beam, which had been taken out of a demolished mill many years before, was introduced. Left exposed and waxed in its natural colour, it looks by no means out of place.

Most of the window sashes proved to be sound: only four needed to be replaced, though for these, special astragals had to be made, standard modern ones being considerably clumsier than those in the other windows. To avoid disturbing the frames the sashes were all hung on spring balances, instead of pulleys and weights. The staircase, of course, is new: a newel post from ground floor to ceiling, besides being structurally necessary, has enhanced its appearance.

The sandstone of which the house is built is soft, and many of the dressed window and door surrounds required patching; but, carefully done, this has proved quite unnoticeable. Two cracked lintels have been strengthened by the insertion of a recessed iron angle, which should give no trouble if kept painted and not allowed to rust. The rubble walls have been rendered with a fairly smooth sand-textured harl following the contours of the stone underneath, and finished white.

Main drainage was expected to be installed in the village within a year or two of this reconstruction, so the sanitary authorities obligingly agreed to a septic tank being built rather nearer the back of the house than the statutory forty feet. The ground at the back, which was banked up almost to sill level in places, has been cut away to form a paved area eight feet wide.

The whole cost of this reconstruction was under £3000 (30s. per square foot at 1951-3 prices), a cost which reflects the standard of equipment (Aga cooker, double sink in stainless steel, built-in cupboards throughout) as well as such minor extravagances as handwrought door latches. To build a house of this size (two public rooms, wide entrance hall, kitchen and bathroom on the ground floor, and five rooms and lavatory upstairs) would not have been permitted at the time; even had it been, the cost would have been well over £4000.

3. House at Kippen, Stirlingshire

The building, part of it reputed to be the oldest in the village, consisted of two cottages in a row running from east to west up the rig at right angles to the road. The eastern part nearer the road – a two-roomed house with a large semi-basement under it – was quite derelict, its roof broken and its interior rotten and indeed dangerous. The other cottage, of two rooms, a small lobby and a closet, had been more recently occupied and was in better condition, though its roof was leaky and some of its walls damp. Both houses were condemned and were to be knocked down to make way for a new road to a projected housing scheme. Fortunately this scheme was dropped, and it was possible to obtain planning consent for reconstruction.

The prospective owner was offered the building and land for £100, but before buying, took advice, first from a builder, who rather optimistically suggested that it could be put in order for about £600, and then from an architect, who made a survey and reported that even with the utmost economy a reconstruction could not be carried out for less than £1,200, and might cost half as much again. A plan for a five-apartment house was drawn up and an application (in principle) made for an improvement grant, but this was unsuccessful. At that time (August 1953) there was a cost ceiling of £800 on work eligible for grant, a restriction which has since been removed.

In the new plan, the principal rooms were placed on the south side to take advantage of the larger existing windows, the open outlook, and the sunshine; and the lobbies and stairs were kept along the north wall. The original entrance to the east house, approached by an outside stair, became the front door, and the entrance to the west house a french window; one of the two entrances to the semi-basement became the kitchen door (fully glazed to light the lobby at the foot of the stairs)

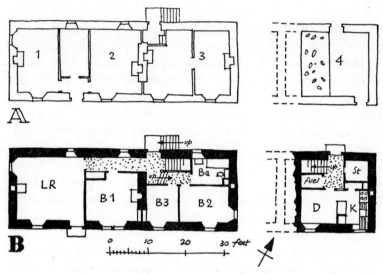

FIG. 35.   House at Kippen, Stirlingshire.

A: Plan before reconstruction. 1 – rotted timber floor; 2 – concrete floor; 3 – suspended floor on point of collapse and roof over very dilapidated; 4 – lower ground floor (? stable) with earth floor partly cobbled.

B: Plan after reconstruction.

and the other was partly built up to form a kitchen window. Three new windows were formed, one to light the bathroom, and the others to improve the lighting of the dining-room and second bedroom to comply with the by-laws. For the same reason the first bedroom window was enlarged into a two-light window. On grounds of economy, cast stone was used for dressings round new openings. The eastern chimney-stack was found to be unsafe and was entirely rebuilt. The other stacks had been rebuilt at a very early date in an attractive local brick: but for re-pointing and minor repairs to the copes they were left untouched and the new stack was built to match them as nearly as possible. A test of the west gable chimney showed that smoke was free to percolate through the stonework and to emerge at many points in the wallhead: this made it necessary to line the flue and to grout the rubble stonework with liquid mortar.

Settlement cracks were visible at the east end of the south elevation, but were found to be of long standing. A wide crack in the old party wall between the cottages caused some anxiety, but here again the fact that the old finishings had been shaped to fit the distorted wall showed that the movement had taken place long ago and had not recurred since.

In repairing the roof, most of the timbers and tiles of the eastern part were renewed. The additional headroom required to make two storeys of habitable rooms out of the old east house was obtained by raising the level of the roof ties, by adjusting the level of the new first floor, and by excavating the semi-basement. The new ground floor was so near foundation level that a certain amount of underpinning of the old walls was necessary.

The first step in damp control was to clear away the earth piled against the west end of the house and to form a trap drain to cut off water flowing down the rig and under the building. Superficially there seemed to be little wrong with the existing boarded floor of the old parlour at this end of the cottage, but upon investigation it was found that the timber bearers resting on the concrete subfloor were rotted. The old floor was removed and a new one (constructed of boarding on bearers and counter-bearers in the manner described in Part 2, in the section on Floors, and ventilated by skirting grilles) was laid on top of bituminous sheeting which formed in effect a damp-proof tray covering the old concrete and extending some

nine inches up the walls behind the skirtings. The rest of the
floor in the west house was of concrete. Where new partitions
were built off it, a felt damp-course, twice the width of the wall,
was first laid on the concrete, and the damp-proofing of the
whole floor was later completed when the cold emulsion adhesive used to fix the thermoplastic-tile floor finish was bonded
to the felt. In the east house the new first floor was supported
on wall bearers fixed to iron corbel pins. In converting the old
semi-basement into a kitchen-dining-room, the outside ground
level was reduced as much as possible, an internal waterproof
tanking was formed under the new concrete floor and carried
up the face of the walls to a height nowhere less than eighteen
inches above outside ground level, and an inner lining of
breeze blocks was built to protect it. All stone walls were
strapped and plastered internally. Outside, the remains of the
old harling were picked off, and since the stonework was soft
and porous it was rendered in lime-cement harling finished
with a wet-dash of lime, cement, and fine whin chips.

The internal finishes were kept very simple. The old doors
and some other finishings from the west house were salvaged
and used again. In that part, about half of the strapped plasterwork was retained, but where the earth piled up against the
building had made the walls damp, the strapping was rotten
and new work was necessary. The ceiling laths and branders
had pulled away from the ties, and after an attempt to save the
old ones had failed, new ceilings in plaster over plasterboard
were provided. Selected red Parana pine was used for the
living-room floor and for the stairs. The kitchen, lobby, and
first bedroom were floored in thermoplastic tiling, and the
floors of the upper bedrooms in softwood left waxed. All new
windows and doors were modelled on the existing ones. The
bathroom door is lined outside to match the boarded doors of
the other rooms, but is finished inside as a flush door with a
sound-proofing core. Ironmongery was chosen from stock
with an eye to simplicity.

Services to the old houses were non-existent, and the contracts for drainage, water-supply, plumber, and electrical works were substantially similar to those for a new house. The grouping of bathroom and kitchen is such that the plumbing and drainage systems are compact and economical. The Rayburn cooker heats both water and a towel-rail in the bathroom. The living-room is heated by a solid fuel stove, and the first bedroom by a small open fire. In both these rooms new fireplaces in timber and quarry-tiles are of a straightforward modern design. The ring-main system with 13-amp outlets was adopted for the electrical supply.

The cost of works was just under £2000, or 32*s*. 6*d*. per square foot of internal area (1953-4 prices).

4. House at Dirleton, East Lothian

Dating from the late seventeenth century, this two-storey farm-house had been considerably altered in later times – first converted into two cottages, and then into two flats with a common wash-house. The County Council acquired it in 1946 and had intended to use the site for new housing. But when the present owner offered to buy it at the District Valuer's valuation, the Council readily agreed and ultimately made a maximum grant of £400, under the Improvement Grants Scheme, towards the cost of reconstructing the property as a family house of seven apartments.

The previous tenants had complained of damp, but this was found to be the result of lack of maintenance rather than inherent faults of construction. Ventilation gratings were blocked with leaves and debris, rones were leaking, down-pipes were split, and the roof needed repair. Damp patches on an internal partition were caused by the coal which had been stored under the stairs. The old harling had disappeared and the rubble stone walls were weathered but still sound. There was no trace of dry rot. Insects had attacked wooden partitions and had damaged the roof timbers, yet not to the point of threatening their stability. Most of the plasterwork and the wood flooring was in fair condition. Main drainage had been laid about thirty years before, and the house was supplied with water and gas but not electricity.

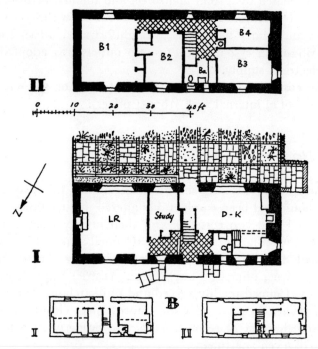

Fig. 36.   Easter Slap, Dirleton.
B: Plans (to half-scale) before reconstruction.

Though serious damp was not apparent, the local authority had to be satisfied that adequate steps had been taken to prevent it. Internal plaster was stripped off up to first-floor level and the stonework was wire-brushed, flushed up in cement mortar, and treated with two coats of damp-resisting compound and plaster bond before re-plastering. The roof

PLATE 15.   EASTER SLAP, DIRLETON

Views of the south front, showing how it has been opened up.
The old wall across the garden now encloses a secluded terrrace
immediately in front of the house. *For Case History, see* p. 131.

PLATE 16. NO. 1 BRIDGE STREET, HADDINGTON

Views of the south front. *For Case History, see* p. 134.

was stripped and the timbers treated with insecticide: then it was sarked with soft-board, felted, and battened. The old pantiles were used again though they had to be eked out with second-hand ones.

The reconstructed house has a large living-room, a study, an L-shaped kitchen-dining room, two double and two single bedrooms, bathroom, and cloakroom. The existing entrance was to the south, and most of the windows faced north. In the reconstruction the planning was reversed: the original north entrance (with lintel dated 1693) was opened again, lobbies were placed on the north side, and large openings were slapped through the south wall to form windows to ground-floor rooms. The solid concrete floor to the dining-room was finished in one-eighth-inch thermoplastic tiles to avoid reducing the existing ceiling height of seven feet. This ceiling height was accepted by the local authority and has proved satisfactory in practice. All other ceilings are eight feet high. Daylighting in the bedrooms is well below minimum standards, but since in two of the four bedrooms there were windows in two walls, the local authority took a lenient and rational view and did not insist on the enlargement of windows.

The sagging joists of the first floor were braced by partitions and a new beam over the living-room, and some of them were reinforced at the bearings by a steel angle fished to the joist and built into the stone wall. The fireplaces on the ground floor were altered to form a boiler recess in the dining-room and an open fireplace in the living-room. The bedroom fireplaces were built up and the flues turned into ventilating shafts by fitting louvres at the bottom and caps at the old chimney cans – a method of ventilation much less costly than slapping openings through the thirty-inch rubble walls. The independent automatic solid fuel boiler supplies hot water to kitchen, cloakroom, and bathroom, and heats the towel-rails. The living-room fire has a back-boiler connected to four radiators which give background heating in the living-room,

K

the hall, and two of the bedrooms. The other two bedrooms and the upper lobby are heated by warm air vents from the airing cupboard. There was an unusally heavy charge of £23 for bringing electricity to the house because it involved rock-cutting. The electrical installation consists of three ring-mains serving 53 socket outlet points – a lavish provision by normal standards but one well worth the slight extra cost.

The floor area of the house is 1552 square feet, and the cost of reconstruction, including built-in cupboards, boiler, radiators, and stainless steel sink unit, but excluding garage and garden works, was £2194, or 29s. per square foot (1955 prices). If some fittings had been omitted and others reduced in quality, there would have been a saving of about 4s. per square foot. The cost of comparable new building would have exceeded £3 per square foot.

5. No. 1 Bridge Street, Haddington, East Lothian

The Waterside area of Haddington was well known to artists at the beginning of the century, when it was teeming with life and lined with old stone buildings facing across the Tyne to St Mary's Church and the open Haugh. Between the wars the houses were neglected and became very overcrowded. Many were demolished by the Town Council during the slum clearance campaign of the 1930's. No. 1 Bridge Street was condemned in 1935 and the four families who were living in it were rehoused, but it was not demolished because it stood hard against the arched approach to the medieval Nungate Bridge. Its gable looks out across the river and forms a fine adjunct to the bridge. Together with a large part of the town it suffered in the 1948 flood, and by 1950 it looked very derelict with its windows crudely blocked by brick and barbed wire, its roof in holes and the abode of many pigeons. In this condition it was acquired for £50.

The house is of two storeys and basement with internal dimensions of 45 by 15 feet. It does not appear to have been harled in the past, and is built of a most colourful variety of local stones and Scots slates. The original house had been sub-divided into a shop and a two-room dwelling on street level

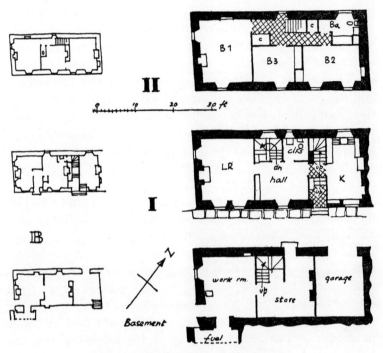

FIG. 37.   Bridge House, Haddington.
B: Plans (to half-scale) before reconstruction.

and a three-room house above, each with a lavatory, sink, and gas lighting. A central brick chimney had been inserted for the cooking ranges. At the time of the acquisition the basement was still used as a store by a dealer in rabbit skins.

The basement, approached direct from Waterside, is built of rounded field stones and probably dates back to the seven-

K I

teenth century. It was clearly unsuitable for habitation but provides admirable space for a garage, workshop, and boiler-room. It also acts as a ventilated space for the house above, obviating the need for a damp-proof course and facilitating the pipe runs from the central heating which has been installed throughout the house. One of the approach archways of the bridge goes with the property and forms a large fuel store.

At street level there were three outside doors. The only one retained is that which led into a tiny lobby and the stair-case to the upper flat: it has become the front door of the re-modelled house. What was the shop door has been blocked up, and the third door, the entrance to the two-room dwelling on the ground floor, has become a window. The little lavatory window and various hatchways from street to basement have also been blocked up. All this patching has been matched with the surrounding wall by using stone from the enlarged opening to the new garage in the basement.

The former shop has become a kitchen, with a dining end by the shop window (converted into an unusually large sash window) and a working end overlooking the garden. It has built-in cupboards and an Aga cooker which also provides domestic hot water. The narrow lobby from which the stair-case ascends has been enlarged by taking down part of the central brick chimney: this has opened up a view through the length of the house and formed an entrance hall of better proportions. The remaining part of the brick chimney has been dressed up with stone. The floor of the lobby had to be renewed: the whole entrance hall is now floored with cork tiles. Beyond it is a dining-hall with a cloakroom off it and a new staircase down to the basement. Beyond that again is the living-room: as well as windows to the south it has a west window looking over the river, and a fine eighteenth-century steel and brass fireplace which was found in the house. None of the ceilings on this floor had to be renewed but they have all been lined with cartridge paper.

The staircase to the top floor was retained, but strengthened by a new stringer. The main bedroom, overlooking the bridge, is a very attractive room with wainscot panelling and shutters. The only necessary renewal was the ceiling, which was done without disturbing a pretty plaster cornice. The other two rooms on this floor were communicating: this had to be altered to make a passageway to a new bathroom at the back, in part of what had been the kitchen. Two small bedrooms were formed with a battery of cupboards between them. This was the only major alteration to the planning of the house. The ceiling height on this floor is nine feet, as it was a later addition to the original structure.

The roof was stripped and found to be basically sound. There was a little woodworm, and weak rafters were reinforced, rotted sarking replaced, the roof felted, slates redressed and rehung. All the windows were renewed as this was estimated to be cheaper than repairing the existing ones. On the other hand all the existing doors were retained, and look well when painted, in spite of minor blemishes. Joists and flooring were of red pine, and apart from the new flooring in the entrance lobby comparatively little patching was necessary. The old floors are slightly uneven, but responded well to sanding. Since there were few signs of internal damp, in spite of the fact that the building had been derelict for some time, it was decided to retain the existing plasterwork, which was directly on the stone, simply patching any broken part instead of going to the expense of stripping it all and strapping and replastering. This economy has proved to be justified on the whole (only in one room has a damp patch persisted, which will probably not be eradicated unless that section of the wall is strapped) but there is no doubt that it involved taking a risk (though a calculated one) particularly when the outside walls were not harled. Not every restorer of an old house who takes the same risk can expect to be equally fortunate.

A policy of retaining the maximum amount of existing work

and only renewing where absolutely necessary has made this a particularly economical restoration. Including a central heating installation the cost was almost exactly 20s. per square foot, if the basement is included in that area. To build a new house of the same area and accommodation in 1950 would have cost two and a half times as much. But the economies have by no means impaired the success of the restoration. The house has proved a most delightful one to live in, with enchanting views all round. It is very warm and economical to run, and it is remarkable how well it has lent itself to mid-twentieth century decoration and way of living.

6. Three Houses at Falkland, Fife

These houses were restored, more or less concurrently, between 1950 and 1953 by Major Michael Crichton-Stuart, Hereditary Keeper of Falkland Palace, and a private society called the Friends of Falkland, formed before the war to arrest the destruction of old houses which was rapidly denuding this ancient burgh of its character. The suspension of the Society's work during the war and immediate post-war years unhappily resulted in the loss of a particularly interesting group of thatched houses in Cross Wynd, the restoration of which was to have been the Society's first operation, but it was still possible to save three old houses in the High Street. Being derelict they were under threat of demolition, but their disappearance would have had a disastrous effect on the precincts of the Palace, for two of them are cheek by jowl with the gate-tower, while the third faces it across the wide street. They contribute much to the simple yet sturdy Scottish burghal character of the setting, so valuable as a foil to the massive Renaissance ornateness of the Royal Palace. These restorations are therefore not only interesting in themselves but exemplary of that comprehensive approach to town design which has been spoken of earlier in this book – an example all the more challenging in that the initiative has not been public but private. Here, as in the reconstruction of Dunkeld by the National Trust for Scotland and the County Council of Perthshire, the vital importance of unpretentious old buildings immediately surrounding a major architectural monument is at last being recognised. Such buildings serve a dual purpose. By their small scale and douce look they throw into stronger relief the already outstanding qualities of the focal building. And they form a buffer between the ancient monument and new building in the vicinity, linking them, bridging the gulf of centuries, while at the same time saving them from discordant proximity.

Moncreif House, on the south side of the High Street facing the Palace, was built in 1610 by Nicoll Moncreif, a member of the personal guard of James VI. The street front, a handsome façade of three storeys in ashlar with moulded dressings at its well-spaced openings, had survived intact; but internally the house had been subdivided and greatly altered: the original newel stair had been removed and another stair built, and the back elevation had been altered to suit. One chimney-head was in bad condition, the roof timbers were decayed, and the thatch dilapidated and verminous.

The house was reconstructed as the residence of a Roman Catholic priest. His housekeeper has rooms on the lower flat, and the upper floor has been planned as a virtually independent flat with its own direct access to the street. On each of these floors one of the existing partitions was retained, together with the great central chimney-stack, and something of the organisation of the original plan was recovered by demolishing the intrusive stair and rebuilding the earlier newel stair. The formal character of the street front forbade any alteration, but the necessary increase of daylighting was readily obtained at the back of the house by reopening blocked-up windows, converting doorways into windows, and by forming new windows.

With some repair, the existing floors were good enough to

retain, and the only considerable area of new flooring was at
the well of the old stair. The original stone fireplace surrounds
and a fine arched aumry (discovered behind strapped plasterwork) were restored. New internal finishings included strapped
plasterwork on all main walls, and joinerwork in a plain
straightforward style. Completely new plumbing and electrical

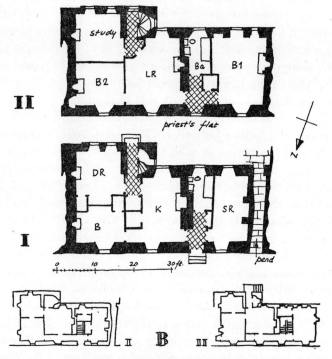

FIG. 38.   Moncreif House, Falkland.
B: Plans (to half-scale) before reconstruction.

systems were installed, and the contract included the painterwork.

One defective gable-head was taken down and rebuilt, and
a completely new roof was constructed and finished in a thatch
of Tay reeds. The thatching was done in traditional Scottish

style by a local craftsman at a cost of about 17s. per yard super,
which compares very favourably with the cost of pantiling; and
with proper maintenance the thatch may be expected to last
a hundred years.

The total accommodation is three public rooms, four bedrooms, kitchen, two bathrooms, and a large attic which has low
wallhead windows in the front of the house. The area within
walls is 1690 square feet with an additional 945 square feet in
the attic. The work was begun late in 1951 and was completed
in 1953 at a cost of £3876. If the attic is reckoned in, the cost
per square foot works out at just under 30s., but perhaps a
truer comparison with other buildings would be obtained if
the attic were taken to be only 50 per cent. useful, bringing out
a rate of 36s. per square foot.

St Andrew's House is the larger of the two on the north side
of the High Street immediately to the west of the Palace gate-
way. It was built in the seventeenth century, but at a later date
a new frontage was built about ten feet in advance of the
original narrow three-storey land, enclosing within the building
the newel stair-tower which had formerly stuck out beyond the
front wall. This frontal addition has made an unusually long
roof on the street elevation, and a great disparity in height
between the front and the back of the house, increased by the
slope of the ground. From the street the house appears to be
only two storeys in height: from the back the windows of the
original three storeys are seen and basement windows as well.

The building had been occupied as three flats, but in the
reconstruction it was decided not to use the top floor as living
accommodation, partly because at the time building materials
were strictly controlled and the other two flats absorbed too
much of the allocation, and partly because the top storey had
only north-facing windows, and south-facing ones could only
have been introduced by breaking the roof, as seen from the
street, with new dormers. The top storey, then, was simply left
as drying space for laundry, while the basement provides a

common wash-house and stores. The two flats have each a
living-room, three bedrooms, kitchen, and bathroom.

The reconstruction involved practically gutting the building.
All the dividing walls (except of course the stone wall which
had been the original front) were removed, and new lath-and-

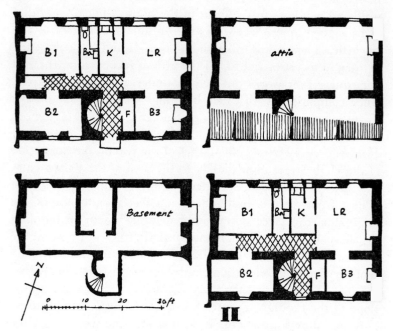

FIG. 39.   St Andrew's House, Falkland.
There were originally only three windows at each floor on the north
front.

plaster partitions formed. External walls were strapped and
plastered. Completely new flooring was put into both flats and
the basement: only in the attic was the old floor considered
good enough to retain. The original newel stair has been repaired. The head of the east gable was in such bad condition
that it had to be taken down: for economy it was rebuilt in
brick, but with the original crowsteps replaced in position. All

the brickwork is harled to match the rest of the house. Eight new windows were formed in the back wall to bring daylighting up to the required standard. The roof was rebuilt but most of the pantiles were saved and used again. New plumbing and electrical systems were provided, and the contract included the painterwork.

The work was carried out between 1950 and 1952 and cost £2973. The area inside external walls (but excluding the thick stone dividing wall) is 1006 square feet per flat. Discounting the attic (full use of which might be a problem in a house of this kind) and making a deduction for the cost of the basement, the cost per flat might be taken as about £1200, or just under 24s. per square foot. Even if the whole cost of the job is charged to the flats alone, the rate per square foot does not rise as high as 30s., which is a remarkable figure considering the extent of the reconstruction and the relatively small amount of habitable space within it. Another point of interest is that final costs in the major trades did not vary from tenders by more than 12 per cent, either way, and that the final cost of the job was 3 per cent under the total of tenders. The architects attribute this to care in allowing for contingencies, and to the skill of a quantity surveyor who was both experienced and interested in this kind of work.

Key House, built in 1713, stands between St Andrew's House and the Palace, its east gable only a few yards from one of the gate-house towers. The street front is simple and spare in the extreme, with few windows in an expanse of plain white walling contrasting with the intricacy of crow-stepped gables and stone-slated roof. On the falling ground behind the main two-storey building is a wing, which was three storeys in height: but during the reconstruction it was reduced to two because the top storey was too low to be of much practical use. The roof of this wing as well as the back half of the main roof are covered in pantiles.

The building, which was in very poor condition, had been in

use as a tenement, but it has been reconstructed as a single house containing two public rooms, two bedrooms, kitchen, bathroom, and a large wash-house. The new plan of the main building retains the simple but-and-ben arrangement of rooms

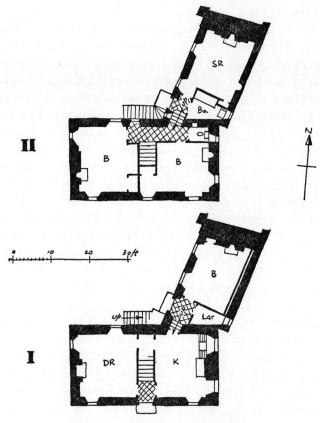

FIG. 40. Key House, Falkland.

flanking a central entrance. The original staircase had to be replaced, a second stair in one corner was removed entirely, but an outside stair in the angle between the main building and the wing was retained, complete with its wooden porch. An opening was slapped to connect the ground-floor kitchen with the wash-house and a new back door. The plumbing was made economical by grouping all sanitary fittings closely together on the two floors. The front elevation was left quite unchanged, the required daylighting of rooms being obtained by new or adapted openings in the gable and back of the house.

New damp-proofing and concrete floors were laid throughout the ground floor, and the side wall of the wash-house (where the ground level is four feet higher than the floor) was made waterproof with a vertical tanking in asphalt carried to a level six inches above ground, backed by an independent lining of brickwork. The solid floors were finished in fleximer composition: the existing upper floors were retained. The roof of the wing was renewed when the top storey was removed, but pantiles were saved from the old roof and eked out with second-hand tiles.

The area within external walls is 1610 square feet, and the cost of works was £2740 or 34s. per square foot, which is about three-fifths of the cost of new building prevailing at the time (1950-2).

Index

References to figures are in *italics*
and those to plates in **bold type**